The Leitrim Trilogy

Callaghan's Place

Unforg

Lovely l

GW00362621

Three Plays by

John McDwyer

ORIGINAL WRITING

Printed by Cahills Printers Limited.
Published by Original Writing Ltd, Dublin, 2010.

for Josephine

John McDwyer was born in Sooey, Co. Sligo in 1947 but describes himself as a naturalised Leitrim man, having lived most of his adult life in that county. He worked in various parts of Ireland for AIB Bank for thirty two years before retiring to help co-found Beezneez Theatre Company, a semi-professional touring company. He has been Artistic Director to the company since it's foundation.

He emerged as a writer in 1992 when his first radio play, Month's Mind, won the RTE PJ O'Connor award and he has had numerous radio plays performed since then. His first published short story, *Fair Day*, won the Leitrim Guardian Literary Award in 1994. Apart from The Leitrim Trilogy, other stage plays include *You'll Never Walk Alone*, *Love is...* and *United*. He lives and works in Carrick on Shannon, Co. Leitrim.

Stage Plays

Lovely Leitrim
You'll Never Walk Alone
Callaghan's Place
Unforgiven
Love is...
United

Radio Plays

Month's Mind
Conacre
On Broken Wings
Isn't the water lovely today?
Watch Masterson
Life for rent

CONTENTS

CALLAGHAN'S PLACE

CHARACTERS

GEORGE DAWSON   Bright young man, late twenties/early thirties.

PAT KELLY   Seen in prologue and epilogue as old man. In the play proper, he is a small dry stock farmer with 30 acres. Aged 55, married to Rita who spends most of her life with a married daughter in England. Also has two sons, both of whom work in Brussels.

PAUL DOLAN   Small, dry stock farmer with 40 acres. Aged 50. Married to Mary. One child, a daughter, Frances.

MARY DOLAN   Wife of Paul. Aged 45. Attractive but careworn.

FRANCES DOLAN   Aged 18. Leaving Certificate Student. Very intelligent and focused. Becoming disappointed with parents.

ANNIE JACKSON   Widowed 60 year old publican. Is also Local Correspondent for weekly newspaper.

THOMAS HOPKINSON   Englishman of indeterminate age (35/45). Very courteous and introverted. The custodian of a great sadness.

3

OUTLINE OF SCENES

The first and last scenes are set sometime in the future.
Otherwise, the play is set in the past.

5

ACT ONE

SCENE ONE

(Prologue)

Sometime in the future.
Annie Jackson's bar. Early afternoon. The bar is almost
derelict. A small table and stool lie on their side. At the
bar, a stool lies on the ground. Grey light.
Dawson enters. He is well dressed with a smart overcoat
and wears a scarf. He looks around the bar, unsure. He
lifts the table and stool, putting them in their proper
place. He takes a handkerchief from his pocket and
wipes the dust from both pieces of furniture. He sits on
the stool and waits, looking around the bar.
A voice is heard outside.

PAT   Hello. Are you there? Where are you?
DAWSON In here. In the bar.
     (To himself)
     I think.
     **Pat Kelly shuffles in. He is an old man but his vitality
     belies his age. Grey hair and moustache. He wears a cap.
     He is carefully rather than stylishly dressed.**
PAT   Hello. I saw the car outside. Are you the man from the
     ah...
DAWSON Yes. Dawson. George Dawson. Are you Mr. Kelly?
PAT   Pat Kelly. Yes. That's me.
DAWSON I'm pleased to meet you.
     They shake hands.
PAT   What the hell brought you in here?

DAWSON	I don't know. I just saw the place and was curious. So I stopped. Wandered in.
PAT	Well, I suppose you're not the first that was enticed into the place.
DAWSON	It was a pub?
PAT	Yeah. Did you not know that?
DAWSON	Well, there's not much sign of it. How would I know?
PAT	Does your crowd not own it? Did ye not buy it with the land?
DAWSON	Was there land adjoining it?
PAT	Arrah, seven or eight acres only.
DAWSON	Well, then we own it. It's just nobody ever mentioned it. I suppose it's not seen as being of any value.
PAT	No. I suppose they'd be waiting for it to fall beyond repair. Then they'd be able to level it.
	Pause.
	Pat lifts the stool, wipes it and sits.
	God, it's a long time since I was in here.
DAWSON	You drank here?
PAT	This was our local. Jackson's. The widow Jackson's.
DAWSON	Your place must be near here so?
PAT	The other side of the bridge.
DAWSON	Ah, yes. I remember the bridge on the map.
PAT	You have no briefcase.
DAWSON	Should I have?
PAT	Oh, I thought all men like you carried briefcases.
DAWSON	For what?
PAT	Who knows? To impress. To look like an expert.
DAWSON	An expert?
PAT	Aye. An expert. Master Flynn, God be good to him, used say that an expert was a man from more than thirty miles away carrying a briefcase.
DAWSON	Well, I'm from more than thirty miles away.
PAT	But you have no briefcase.
DAWSON	No. So what does that make me?
PAT	Dangerous.
DAWSON	Dangerous?
PAT	Yes. I could sabotage what you'd have in a briefcase but

I can't pilfer out of your head.

Pause.

DAWSON Was this a good pub?

PAT I don't know. How do you measure pubs? It served us well.

DAWSON Long closed?

PAT Since the widow died. Her nephew sold the licence and then your crowd must have bought the rest.

DAWSON There must have been quite a few people living up here onetime when it merited a pub.

PAT Ah, one time. There was nearly as many people then as there's trees now.

DAWSON Where did they all go?

PAT Died. Anyone that didn't die, left. Went to live in the real world.

DAWSON Real world?

PAT Arrah, got married somewhere else or got work away from the land.

DAWSON I see.

PAT Are you married yourself?

DAWSON No. At least not yet.

PAT Time enough.

DAWSON Time enough.

PAT Indeed'n you might be time enough if you never got married.

DAWSON You think?

PAT Isn't it a remarkable thing that neither God nor his Son ever got married? Do you think they knew something that the rest of us didn't?

DAWSON Could be. Well, to work. I gather I have two missions here. To talk to you about your place...

PAT *(Interrupting)*
Again.

DAWSON Again. And I'd like you to show me Dolan's house and Callaghan's place.

PAT Callaghan's place?

DAWSON Yes.

PAT What's to be seen at Callaghan's place? Isn't it planted?

9

DAWSON	The house.
PAT	What house?
DAWSON	Callaghan's.
PAT	Sure that's gone.
DAWSON	Gone?
PAT	Aye. Burned. There's nothing there only the leavings of walls.
DAWSON	When was it burned?
PAT	Years ago.
DAWSON	It's still on the map.
PAT	Maybe it is. Seeing this place isn't, I wouldn't pass much heed of maps.
DAWSON	Anyway, I'd better go and take a look.
PAT	Suit yourself, but there's nothing to see.
DAWSON	How did it happen?
PAT	What?
DAWSON	The fire. The burning.
PAT	No one knows for sure.
DAWSON	Come on. Everyone knows everything in a place like this.
PAT	Maybe. A shut mouth, Mr. Dawson, swallows no flies.
DAWSON	You're not going to tell me anyway.
PAT	Why do you think that?
DAWSON	Oh, I just thought you'd say it was none of my business.
PAT	Neither it is. Did they never tell you in Head Office?
DAWSON	What would they know about here? They obviously don't even know that the place was burned.
	Pause.
	God, how can you stay here?
PAT	Why? How do you mean?
DAWSON	The place is so desolate. So quiet.
PAT	Maybe I like it that way.
DAWSON	How the hell did people live here?
PAT	Happily, most of them. Even a candle tries it's best the length it's lit. I could take you to a rock at the top of this place and show you the remains of sixteen houses below us.
	Loughlin's.

	Farrell's.
	Clancy's.
	Brady's. The ceilidh house.
DAWSON	Ceilidh house?
PAT	Aye. There was a big family in Bradys. Every one of them musical. Christ, even the sewing machine in that house was a singer.
DAWSON	All left.
PAT	All left.
DAWSON	Except Mr. Patrick Kelly.
PAT	Except me.
	Pause.
	C'mon. We'll start at Dolan's. I'd better tell you the story.
DAWSON	What story?
PAT	About Callaghan's place.
DAWSON	You're going to tell me? Why?
PAT	Because, Mr. Dawson, you're a curious man and if I don't tell you you'll enquire in Carrick and you'll be told a heap of shite and rumours. And that wouldn't be fair to either the living or the dead.
DAWSON	I see.
PAT	So, anyway, the time it happened, the Callaghan brothers were after dying within a year of each other and the place had been empty for a while. Paul and Mary Dolan were in their place, where we're going now, with their daughter, Frances.
	(Showing Dawson out)
	After you.
DAWSON	And you were?
PAT	I was where I still am.

THEY EXIT AS LIGHT FADES
CROSS FADE LIGHT TO SCENE TWO

SCENE TWO

The kitchen of the Dolan household. It is a neat farmhouse with little beyond the essentials. Sink unit, with side cabinet and drawer, formica-topped table and chairs. Paul and Mary Dolan and their daughter, Frances, are finishing breakfast. It is the first day of school following the Easter holiday.

MARY	There's more porridge in the pot, Frances, if you want some.
PAUL	And leave her late for the bus.
FRANCES	Arrah, I have tons of time.
PAUL	You have. You always have tons of time 'till you have no time and then I have to drop every thing and leave you into the school when you miss the bus.
FRANCES	When did you have to do that?
PAUL	The Monday after St. Patrick's Day, hadn't I to do it?
FRANCES	Once. I suppose I'll never hear the end of that.
MARY	Will ye give it a break, the two of ye.
PAUL	Well I have more to be doing with my time than be running here and there with one that can't get up in time to catch the bus.
MARY	Will we have to listen to this every morning 'till the end of June?
FRANCES	Well, you won't hear it again after that, I can promise you.
	Pause
PAUL	Anyway, I'll check the bike.
MARY	It's checked. C'mon. Frances. Some morning you'll get a puncture and the bus won't wait for you at the end of the road.
FRANCES	That's symbolic.
PAUL	What?
FRANCES	Everybody 'round here misses the bus sooner or later.
MARY	Will you be late home?

FRANCES	No. I'm finished at four so I'll be on the first bus. Oh, hi, I see smoke rising from Callaghan's place this morning. The new man must have moved in.
PAUL	He moved in yesterday.
FRANCES	What's he like?
PAUL	I was only talking to him for a minute. He seems a civil enough kind of a being.
MARY	He's English.
FRANCES	How do you know that? Has he a long tail on him and horns growing out of his head.
PAUL	Don't be so smart with your mother, you.
FRANCES	Sorry, Ma. It's just the way you said it like as if it was a disease. What age is he?
PAUL	How do I know? I didn't ask him for his passport.
FRANCES	*(mocking)* Well, you should have. You need to check these people out. We can't be letting every auld bit of riffraff into Paradise, you know. You're no good for the news. I'll drop in on the way home from school and chat him up.
MARY	You will not.
FRANCES	Why not?
PAUL	Don't be going in anywhere you're not invited.
FRANCES	You went in.
PAUL	That was different. I was bringing a creel of turf for his first fire.
FRANCES	Well, sure I can bring a six pack for his first party.
MARY	Frances.
FRANCES	A joke. No, seriously, I'll just put my head around the door to say hello.
PAUL	He strikes me as a man that would like his own company.
FRANCES	That's only because he hasn't had the pleasure of mine. **She takes schoolbag from back of chair, grabs slice of toast from mother's plate and exits.** I'll see yiz.
MARY	Take it easy on that bike.
FRANCES	*(From outside)* I will.

13

PAUL	Take it easy on that bike. You might as well be talking to Stephen Roche.
MARY	Can the pair of ye not stop picking at each other?
PAUL	Who's picking?
MARY	You're too alike.
PAUL	How?
MARY	In your ways. Like two peas in a pod.
PAUL	Well she won't be here much longer to pick at. **Pause** Did she say what she's doing for the summer?
MARY	I don't know. I suppose she'll be in the chipper again.
PAUL	**Goes to door and looks out** There she goes, down the hill like the hammers of hell.
MARY	She'll get tossed off that bike yet.
PAUL	Starting the last term. God, it's hard to believe. Eighteen gone. And she's nearly finished. Leaving. Where do the years go at all?
MARY	Aye. She's going.
PAUL	What'll we do? What will become of us?
MARY	What's wrong with you, Paul. You spend half your time fighting with her and now you don't want her to go.
PAUL	It's not that I don't want her to go. I know she has to go. There was no point in her schooling if she don't go. Education isn't going to come into her here. It's just I never thought of the place without her.
MARY	And what'll happen to us? God, you'd think 'twas two old age pensioners was in it. What'll happen to us only what always happened to us. We'll work like dogs for nothing and we'll get no thanks for it from anyone. But sure didn't we always know that would be the case. What else was ever before us?
PAUL	I'd be happier if she didn't go into that man 'till she's asked.
MARY	Why? What's wrong with him?
PAUL	He's kinda reserved looking. You wouldn't know what way he'd take it.
MARY	Did you ask him up?
PAUL	Of course I did. And I told him I'd bring him down to

	Annie's for a drink some night. I think he's going in
	there today anyway with an ad for the Observer.
MARY	An ad?
PAUL	Aye. He's trying to set the few acres.
MARY	He'll be lucky with that scrub.
PAUL	I warned him that goats don't read the paper.
MARY	It's no good to us?
PAUL	Arrah, devil a bit. We have enough.
MARY	I suppose. Do you want the car this morning?
PAUL	No. Why?
MARY	I want to go into Carrick to see about material for
	curtains.

He looks.

We have the station. Remember?

PAUL   Oh, aye. Well off with you so. I'll clear these things
        away.

**Mary takes keys from the side of the dresser and exits.
Paul begins to clear the table and place dishes in the
sink. Paul hesitates for a second.**

Symbolic. I wonder what the hell does that mean?

**He opens a drawer at the sink. He takes out a small
dictionary and flicks through it until he finds a word.**

Symbolic. Symbol. Sign or thing that stands for
something else.

He repeats.

Sign or thing that stands for something else.

CROSS FADE TO BAR

SCENE THREE

Annie Jackson's bar. Mid morning. An old bar. It is the
bar seen in the prologue now seen as a working bar.
Pat Kelly sits at the counter. He has a glass in front of
him containing one quarter of it's original pint. He and
Annie Jackson, the bar owner, are doing a crossword.

ANNIE   Can you block him with the basket?
PAT   Can you block him with the basket?
ANNIE   Yes.
PAT   How many letters?
ANNIE   Six. And R is the last one.
PAT   The basket. The basket. I have it. Hamper. A picnic
          basket.
ANNIE   Good man, Pat. We're going well the day.
          **Thomas Hopkinson enters. Pat and Annie stop to look
          at him. He approaches Annie nervously.**
THOMAS   Mrs. Jackson?
ANNIE   Yes.
THOMAS   Oh, good. They tell me that I can place a small
          advertisement in the Observer with you.
ANNIE   You can. Yes.
THOMAS   Good. I have it written out here. You might check if it's
          alright.
ANNIE   *(Reading)*
          Sixteen acres of good quality land to let for three years.
          Contact...
PAT   *(Interrupting)*
          Begod, you're the man that's after buying Callaghan's
          place.
THOMAS   Yes. That's right.
PAT   You're very welcome.
THOMAS   Thank you.
PAT   *(Shaking hands)*
          Pat Kelly. I own the land on the other side of the bridge

	from yourself and Paul Dolan. This is Mrs. Jackson, Annie Jackson and happy days to you.
THOMAS	Well, thank you very much.
PAT	Whats'is your name is?
THOMAS	Hopkinson. Thomas Hopkinson.
PAT	Well, there's one thing sure, Thomas Hopkinson, there'll be no mistaking you around here. If there's anyone looking for Mr. Hopkinson he won't be asked which Hopkinson would you be looking for?
THOMAS	No. That's true.
PAT	When did you arrive?
THOMAS	Just yesterday. I...
PAT	*(Interrupting)* Tell us. How much did you pay for the place? There's different reports. I'd say you wouldn't have much change out of twenty thousand.
THOMAS	Well, I...
PAT	Hah?
THOMAS	I really...
PAT	*(Interrupting)* 'Salright. A nod is as good as a wink. Can I get you a drink?
THOMAS	Well it's a bit early in the day for me.
PAT	Ah, just to welcome you. You'll play a poor tune on a dry whistle.
THOMAS	Well, maybe a bottle of beer? Would that be alright?
PAT	That would be game ball. And a half one for me, Annie. Where did you come from, Mr. Hopkinson?
THOMAS	England. And it's Thomas.
PAT	Surely. What part of England?
THOMAS	Well, Chelmsford was my last...Chelmsford.
PAT	Chelmsford. God, ye have lovely names on places in England. Hah? Fakenham. Fontwell. Newtown Abbot. Uttoxeter.
THOMAS	Pontefract.
PAT	What?
THOMAS	Pontefract. I gather you are a follower of race horses.
ANNIE	Not at all, Mr. Hopkinson. You don't have to follow

17

	the horses Pat backs at all. You can run past them anytime.
PAT	As well as being our publican, Thomas, Annie is also our local comic.
THOMAS	I see. Yes.
PAT	What are you going doing above in Callaghan's place?
THOMAS	Well, I don't know, really. Apart from knowing that I won't be farming. I'll keep the garden.
PAT	And what were you at in England?
THOMAS	Oh, this and that. You know.
PAT	Indeed'n I do well. Amn't I at it all my life. Are you married?
THOMAS	No. I haven't had the pleasure.
ANNIE	Nor the pain. You'll excuse me a minute. I'll phone in this ad for you.

(exiting)

	I'll put a welcome to you in the local notes as well so that people will know who you are. If that's alright?
THOMAS	Yes, that would be nice. Thank you, Mrs. Jackson.

Annie exits.

	She seems a very pleasant lady.
PAT	Oh, Annie is grand. Only one thing you need to watch with Annie. She'd go up your arse for news.
THOMAS	And Mr. Jackson?
PAT	Dead. Annie is a widow these ten years at least. God love her, she hadn't it aisy. She spent her youth in England, looking after an auld aunt and when she died she had to come home and look after her own auld pair. You'd think, after that, she'd be entitled to a husband.
THOMAS	And she didn't re-marry.
PAT	Arrah, no. But I suppose she could yet. You often seen a horse running twice in the Grand National. She's a bit like P J Gallagher's Peugeot, body wrecked but a great auld engine in her.
THOMAS	And yourself?
PAT	Me?
THOMAS	You're married?

PAT	I'm still serving time. Although I see so little of her these times I might as well be a widow.
THOMAS	Oh?
PAT	We have a daughter in England. Married. To an Englishman.
THOMAS	Oh, really?
PAT	Yes. You hardly? Ah, you wouldn't know them.
THOMAS	Whereabouts do they live?
PAT	Birmingham. Is that far from Chelmsford?
THOMAS	A fair bit. Yes.
PAT	I suppose. Anyway, what part of Ireland are you from?
THOMAS	I'm not. I'm from England. I was born in Ashford, in Kent.
PAT	You might have been born over there but you're Irish. Everyone is Irish. Did you not know that?
THOMAS	Not in my case. No. I don't think so.
PAT	You trace yourself back and you'll find a Paddy and a Biddy lying together on some branch of the family tree.
THOMAS	I don't think so.
PAT	Sure Adam was an Irishman.
THOMAS	Good Lord, where did you get that notion?
PAT	I'm telling you. Himself and Eve are in the garden. She's horsing into the apple and your man is foostering around with the fig leaf. She's feeling a bit frisky and says, 'hi, Adam, do you want a bit?' And the eejit, probably from Cavan, thinks she's talking about the apple and the bollox takes a bite and banjaxes the rest of us for eternity.
THOMAS	*(Laughing)* It's certainly an unusual slant on the story.
PAT	Well, I'll tell you, Thomas, if it's not true, it should be.
THOMAS	You spoke of your wife being away a lot. Why is that?
PAT	Arrah, the daughter that's married in Birmingham. She has a child and my woman goes over to mind the child during school times. She comes back here for the holidays.
THOMAS	Oh, I see. Your daughter is a school teacher?

19

PAT	She works in a school. Yeah.
THOMAS	Have you sons?
PAT	Two. Both of them beyond in Brussels. The eldest lad is working with a computer. He's doing well. The second lad is portering in a hotel. He says he's trying to find himself.
THOMAS	Find himself?
PAT	I hope he has better luck than me. I could never find the hoor when he was here. You have good neighbours up there, Thomas.
THOMAS	Oh yes. I met Paul, is it Paul Dolan?
PAT	Aye.
THOMAS	He seems a very decent gentleman.
PAT	Well, now, you've just described him to a tee. And the same description fits the wife and daughter. Except, of course that they're not gentlemen.
	Annie returns.
ANNIE	Now, I've done that for you, Mr. Hopkinson.
THOMAS	Please, Thomas. How much is it?
ANNIE	Ten eighty.
THOMAS	Fine.
	(Proffering twenty euro note)
	And may I buy a drink for my friend, Pat, here?
ANNIE	Oh, you may. I doubt if Pat will stand between you and the counter waving a baseball bat.
PAT	Good manners prevents my refusal, Thomas. A pint.
ANNIE	And yourself?
THOMAS	No, thank you. I left a fire lighting so I'd best get back.
PAT	We'll see you again soon, I hope?
THOMAS	Yes. Well, Paul, my neighbour offered to bring me down for a drink some night. I'll look forward to that.
ANNIE	*(giving change)*
	Good. Well, we'll see you then.
THOMAS	Cheerio.
PAT	Good luck.
	Thomas exits.
	Pause
ANNIE	Do you want that pint now, Pat?

PAT	No. Leave it for tonight.
	Pause
	Funny fish.
ANNIE	How?
PAT	Hard to get anything out of him. You wouldn't know what to make out of him.
ANNIE	He seems quite nice.
PAT	It didn't take him long to get in on the craic here.
ANNIE	How do you mean?
PAT	Did you hear the ad? Good quality land?
ANNIE	What about it?
PAT	Good quality me arse. The snipes built a by-pass round that place years ago.
ANNIE	It's not that bad, is it?
PAT	Hah? He'll get no farmer to take that place. His only chance is a sailor.
ANNIE	Anyway, it's good to see Callaghan's place lived in again. Mary Dolan will be glad of the company.
PAT	Oh, begod, she will. Better looking fella than either of the two bucks that was in it, too.
ANNIE	Yes, well I'm sure that won't be of much interest to Mary.
PAT	No. I suppose. Tell me, Annie, how sure are you of that?
ANNIE	Will she sing for her supper?
PAT	What?
ANNIE	Will she sing for her supper? Seven letters.

CROSS FADE TO THOMAS' KITCHEN

SCENE FOUR

Thomas Hopkinson's kitchen. Essential furnishings
are small kitchen table and two chairs. The farmhouse
kitchen of two old bachelor brothers, which it
was, until recently. The table is strewn with the
paraphernalia of a writer. Small portable typewriter.

Thomas enters, through fade up, speaking on mobile
phone.

THOMAS   No, fine. Very good, in fact and a lot better than I
          expected. Thank you for calling. I'll call you in a few
          days.
          He sits at the table and begins typing.
          Frances enters.
FRANCES   I'm sorry. I did knock. You mustn't have heard me with
          the racket on the typewriter.
THOMAS   Oh, yes. Of course. I'm sorry.
FRANCES   No, I'm sorry. I shouldn't have torn in unannounced.
          My father is always giving out to me for going places
          I'm not invited. I'm Frances, by the way. No, not
          Frances By the Way. Frances Dolan. Up the road. You
          met my father yesterday evening.
THOMAS   Oh yes. Yes, indeed. Frances, I'm very pleased to meet
          you. Frances with an e.
FRANCES   Yeah. I think my father wanted a son and that was the
          nearest he could get to it.
THOMAS   Please, won't you sit down? Can I get you something?
          Tea? Coffee, perhaps? I'm afraid I'm not too well
          organised as yet.
FRANCES   Thanks for the offer but no. I'll be having the dinner
          when I go home. I'm on my way home from school.
THOMAS   You go to school in town?
FRANCES   In Carrick, yeah. I'm doing the leaving this year.

THOMAS	Leaving?
FRANCES	Oh, of course, you wouldn't know anything about that. It's the GSE or the GAA or something in England, isn't it?
THOMAS	The GCSE. That's the first exam and then there's A levels.
FRANCES	Yeah. Well that's what I'm at. In June.
THOMAS	And what are your intentions afterwards?
FRANCES	I want to go to university. In Dublin. To study law.
THOMAS	Well done. A good ambitious choice.
FRANCES	And yourself?
THOMAS	Sorry?
FRANCES	What are your plans? What in the name of God are you doing in a dump like this?
THOMAS	Well, Frances, I'm here less than a day. I'll make it tidier in time.
FRANCES	I'm not talking about the house. The place. The area.
THOMAS	It seems very peaceful to me. Almost idyllic.
FRANCES	It's peaceful alright. Dead as a door nail.
THOMAS	We're obviously looking for different things. It's very suitable for me at this point in time.
FRANCES	You're a writer?
THOMAS	Well, I'm hoping to be.
FRANCES	What kind of stuff do you write? Books? Poetry?
THOMAS	Actually, I'm attempting to write a play.
FRANCES	A play? What's it about? Is it an Irish play?
THOMAS	Well, it's about leaving. Going away.
FRANCES	It's an Irish play, so.
THOMAS	Since Pat, whom I met in the tavern earlier, almost convinced me that I am Irish; I should be able to write an Irish play.
FRANCES	So you met Pat Grant, did you?
THOMAS	No. I believe Pat Kelly was his name.
FRANCES	No, that's Pat Grant. Oh, Pat Kelly is his real name but he's called Pat Grant because he knows every grant that's going for anything. He should, too. He has collected most of them.
THOMAS	Really?

FRANCES	Yeah. The latest one my auld fella came home with one night was ostrich farming. Did you ever hear the beat of that? Pat Grant had figured out there was great money in it from Europe.
THOMAS	Ostrich farming?
FRANCES	Honest to God. Sure if an ostrich stuck his head in the ground 'round here he'd never get it out again. He'd get bogged.
THOMAS	Bogged?
FRANCES	Stuck. You haven't got the vernacular yet, have you? **Pause.** By the way, you didn't introduce yourself.
THOMAS	Oh, my. How ill-mannered of me. Thomas. Thomas Hopkinson.
FRANCES	Thomas Hopkinson. Very English, I think. What were you at in England, Thomas?
THOMAS	Oh, this and that.
FRANCES	Mind your own business, Francie.
THOMAS	No, it's just...
FRANCES	Don't mind. Keep it to yourself. It'll be a bit of a challenge for Pat and the widow.
THOMAS	The widow?
FRANCES	Annie Jackson. The publican.
THOMAS	Oh yes. I met her. Nice lady.
FRANCES	Yes. She is. So, anyway, an Englishman who won't say what he was doing in England arrives and takes over Callaghan's Place. Very mysterious. Very...
THOMAS	English?
FRANCES	Yes. What's'is our teacher says about the English? Oh, yes, *(quoting)* 'From this amphibian, ill born mob began, That vain ill-natured thing, an Englishman.' I think our teacher is a bit of a Republican.
THOMAS	Daniel Defoe.
FRANCES	Sorry?
THOMAS	The quotation is from Daniel Defoe. 'The True Born Englishman' is the name of the piece.

FRANCES	Is it?
THOMAS	Yes. In it he also says *(quoting)* 'Wherever God erects a house of prayer The devil always builds a chapel there. And 'twill be found, upon examination, The latter has the largest congregation.'
FRANCES	The devil has all the best tunes.
THOMAS	Yes, I suppose that would sum it up. But you don't believe that, do you?
FRANCES	Well, he mightn't have the best tunes but he has the most popular ones.
THOMAS	What an extraordinary observation. I see that I shall have to be careful with you.
FRANCES	Have you met my ma?
THOMAS	Yes, she called this morning. On her way back from the town. And she has invited me to visit.
FRANCES	For God's sake, you don't need an invitation to visit us. We're only up the road; sure the Callaghans were in and out the whole time, day and night.
THOMAS	That's a thing that puzzles me.
FRANCES	What?
THOMAS	How did those two brothers live on a farm this size?
FRANCES	Sure they didn't. Didn't they die?
THOMAS	Yes, but that wasn't what killed them.
FRANCES	Of course it was. Ok, I know Stephen was found in a shed with a heart attack and Robert caved in from loneliness inside a year but sure it was hunger and drudgery brought all that on. The place killed them.
THOMAS	But that won't happen to you?
FRANCES	You can type that in block capitals on your typewriter, Thomas. I'm working hard to get into college. That's my ticket out of this place.
THOMAS	Always buy a return ticket. You never know when you might want or need to come back.
FRANCES	I see that I shall have to be careful with you, too, Thomas. Anyway, I'll be seeing you.
THOMAS	You will call again? Whenever you wish.

FRANCES	Words, Thomas, that you will live to regret. I'll make a pit stop every day on my way home. Eventually, I'll know everything about you. I'll beat Pat Grant to it.
THOMAS	I'm afraid you won't find the information very interesting.
FRANCES	Let me be the judge of that.
THOMAS	It's been lovely meeting you, Frances.
FRANCES	And you, Thomas. You know, I've a feeling we'll be great mates. See you.
	She exits.

Thomas goes to exit point and looks after Frances as lights cross fade to Annie's Bar.

SCENE FIVE

Annie's Bar. Pat and Annie are in conversation. It is early night.

ANNIE	But what can ye do about it?
PAT	Can't we show them that at least we're united?
ANNIE	But if it's true what you say, that Europe wants to get rid of the small farmer, what's the point in fighting it?
PAT	God, Annie, you haven't an ounce. Sure if we take it lying down we'll get nothing out of it. If they want us out, that's fine, but we should make sure that they pay for it.
ANNIE	How?
PAT	Grants. Subsidies. Sure them fellas in Brussels think they're doing mighty work. Buying us off. Firing money at us. And the poor auld hoors don't realise that we were going anyway. Disappearing. If they had patience, they'd get us for nothing.
ANNIE	So what are ye doing tonight. What's this, what is it ye're forming?
PAT	A study group. I got the idea from the Journal. We can get a grant to run it.
ANNIE	And what are ye going to study?
PAT	Europe.
ANNIE	Europe?
PAT	Europe.
ANNIE	And Europe is studying ye?
PAT	You may be sure of it.
ANNIE	Wouldn't it save a lot if ye met half way, maybe in London and ye could have a good look at each other?
PAT	Oh, you can laugh, Annie but mark my words. It's the screeching wheel that gets oiled.
ANNIE	Sometimes, Pat, I think you have a bit of a persecution complex.
PAT	Did you ever notice in the Auction ads, in the

27

	list of goods at the end when they have listed all the important things they finish with 'and other miscellaneous objects.'
ANNIE	Yes, what about it?
PAT	We're the miscellaneous objects of Europe. The etceteras. That's why it's important to be in a group. Brussels don't like groups. A group gives them the impression they're dealing with intelligent people. They know then we're people that can't be convinced by logical argument alone. We have to be bought. **Thomas and Paul enter.**
THOMAS	Good evening, Pat. Annie.
ANNIE	Thomas. Paul.
PAT	Well, men. Drink?
PAUL	I'll have a half one
PAT	Thomas?
THOMAS	A beer will be grand.
PAT	Suas, Annie.
PAUL	*(indicating folder on the counter)* That's very official looking, Pat.
PAT	There's no point going near these fellas unless you look like you mean business. Now, bucko, second anything I propose in case any of these gobshites try to stop us from starting the group.
PAUL	I will, Pat.
PAT	Good man.
PAUL	What bloody use is it going to be anyway?
PAT	Sure we won't know that 'till we get tore into it. And if we don't do it aren't we just leaving the grant lying there. Are you coming down, Thomas?
THOMAS	No, Pat, I have nothing to contribute. I'll remain here and keep Annie company.
PAT	Oh, begod, we'll have that all over the town by night. D'Englishman and the widow are keeping company.
ANNIE	You'd better not or you'll have to go the bank to cash your next cheque.
PAUL	You needn't worry yourself, Annie. He's not going to go near the bank with any cheques.

PAT	It's alright for you, Paul. The bank manager calls you by your first name. All I get is Mr. Kelly. 'We haven't seen you for quite some time, Mr. Kelly.'
THOMAS	Are you having some difficulty with the bank, Pat?
PAT	Well to be honest with you, Thomas, no. But the bank seems to be having some difficulty with me.
ANNIE	They're a bit unreasonable. They want him to pay them back.
PAT	And I will too, when I have it. If I ever have it.
THOMAS	Have you tried sitting down with them. Sometimes it helps if...
PAT	*(interrupting)* Sitting down with them? Sure I'm a sitting duck altogether if I do that. The last time I was in, the wife was home at the time and sent me in when she saw all the letters on the mantle-piece. Your buck is within, the colour of clarinda after coming back from Florida. 'Well, Mr. Kelly' says he 'how are we going to get out of this mess?' 'Well, to tell you the truth' says I, 'you don't look like a man that's in much of a mess at all.' Well, he opened on me. The two barrels I got. In the end I had to say to him 'lookit, stall the digger a second. The wife is home so I can get any God's own amount of abuse in my own house for nothing—I don't have to come in here and pay for it' and got up and walked out.
ANNIE	And what happened?
PAT	Oh, the usual. Another letter threatening law.
THOMAS	Law? That's serious.
PAT	Arrah, not at all. By the time they'd have the paperwork done; Paul's Frances would be qualified to defend me.
PAUL	Wouldn't you be better to give him something, meet him half way?
PAT	And haven't I signed over two grants to them. The one from the Heritage Council for the thatching and one of my headages.
PAUL	You don't have any problem like that, Thomas.

THOMAS	Thankfully, no. I can manage to pay my way.
PAT	Oh, I can manage to pay my way, too, Thomas. It's paying everyone else's way that has me banjaxed.
THOMAS	What do you mean?
PAUL	Small wife and a large family.
THOMAS	But I understood they were, what way do you say it, finished.
PAT	Finished?
THOMAS	Yes. Working. Finished.
PAUL	Hah! God help your wit, Thomas.
PAT	What do you call yer man in the Bible, you know the fella that God asked to kill his own son as a sacrifice?
THOMAS	Abraham.
PAT	Aye. That's the buck. Well, when he's telling the wife what the boss is after asking him to do and she's bawling and roaring about losing the son and you know the way you'd be, thinking you should be saying something but not knowing what to say so yer man says to the wife 'look on the bright side, won't it be one of them finished?'
ANNIE	That's shocking, Pat. You're embarrassing poor Thomas.
THOMAS	I have never met anyone with such twists on religious experiences.
PAUL	Ah, but Pat has studied religion.
THOMAS	What? In the priesthood or what?
PAT	Don't heed that hoor. He's only winding you up. Maybe he's fishing for information…
THOMAS	But if that's the case, Paul, I mean if they are never finished, you'll be stuck in the bank the same as Pat by the time Frances has her law degree.
PAUL	Don't you once worry about Frances. We'll be well fit to pay for whatever she wants to do.
ANNIE	I don't think Thomas meant that.
THOMAS	No. No offence meant, Paul. I was merely trying to make a joke.
PAUL	No offence taken. It's not something I'd joke about. She's all we have and we'll look after her.

THOMAS	Indeed. And well looked after she obviously is. She's very bright. Very...optimistic. Yes, optimistic.
ANNIE	That's unusual around here.
PAUL	I wouldn't want anyone putting notions in her head.
THOMAS	No, of course not. I can appreciate that.
PAT	*(lifting folder)* C'mon Paul. We'll be late.
PAUL	Alright. *(to Thomas)* I'll collect you later.
THOMAS	Fine. Thank you, Paul.
PAT	*(exiting)* Now, don't forget, second anything I propose.
PAUL	I will. I will. **They exit.** **Pause**
THOMAS	I think I'll have a second beer, Annie.
ANNIE	Second beer, Thomas? You're becoming native.
THOMAS	I feel I have some distance to come yet before I'm native. Was it my imagination or did I hear a warning shot go across my bows just now?
ANNIE	Are you close to the daughter?
THOMAS	Frances?
ANNIE	Yes.
THOMAS	Well, yes. I suppose I am. And, indeed, to Mary. And Paul. They're excellent neighbours. I mean I'm only two months here and it seems much longer, I have been so well accepted.
ANNIE	Yes. Well that's the way of them. It would be in their nature to be good neighbours.
THOMAS	And Frances is an extraordinary girl. Really intelligent. She makes me laugh. Anything she doesn't know, she wants to know. Very questioning without being inquisitive.
ANNIE	I think Paul is finding it hard going with her.
THOMAS	Paul? Her father?
ANNIE	Oh, maybe I'm wrong. It was just something Mary said when I was talking to her the time of the station in the

	house. Something about Frances passing them out and Paul not being able to keep up.
THOMAS	Intellectually, you mean?
ANNIE	Well that and as well, you have to understand, Paul is from a man's world, a man's work. He wouldn't know how to handle a daughter. Especially one that would stand up to him.
THOMAS	Yes?
ANNIE	Arrah, she's always going on about the place being a dive and she can't wait to get out of it. That can't go easy on a man that spent all his life working at the place, working for her. And now all the value she'll leave on it is that it provides the money to get her out of it. That can't be easy.
THOMAS	No, I can see that. Do you think I should have a word with Frances? Could I do any good?
ANNIE	Maybe. But you'd want to time that right, too. If she thought anyone was behind it she'd kick up the traces. For all her brightness and intelligence she's just like Paul behind it all, thick as a ditch when she wants to be.
THOMAS	You have a great insight into people around here, Annie.
ANNIE	God knows, I should have. Amn't I looking at them long enough?
THOMAS	Why do you continue? Do you never get tired? Feel like doing something else?
ANNIE	Like what? Sure what else do I know? I can hardly throw it up and go lecturing on rocket science, can I? I never got much chance to do anything else. When I left school, I went to England to look after an aunt that was supposed to last six months and she went eleven years, I had to come home here then to see my own parents off. When they died I was left with the place and I'm here since and will be 'till I die and then a nephew above in Dublin who couldn't care less about the place will conduct an auction on the lid of my coffin and the chalice will pass to some other poor

	devil.
THOMAS	Chalice?
ANNIE	Ah, that's a bit unfair, I suppose. Most of the time I enjoy it. It's a bit depressing sometimes, when things aren't going great for the likes of Pat Grant but most of the time it's alright.
THOMAS	That is a most peculiar relationship Pat has with his bank manager, I must say.
ANNIE	You wouldn't want to pay too much attention to that, Thomas. Pat is inclined to exaggerate his poverty.
THOMAS	Why should he do that?
ANNIE	Who knows? It would take a master jeweller to explain the workings of that clock. Pat is like a corncrake. You can hear him all the time but you can never figure out what field he's in. And anyway, for all his moaning he's too good-natured for his own good.
THOMAS	Yes?
ANNIE	He's the kind of man that if the Government bought a drink for the nation, he'd feel it his duty to buy the second round. You're well settled into Callaghan's Place?
THOMAS	Indeed. If I could get the land let I would have no problems.
ANNIE	Any offers?
THOMAS	Not one. Paul offered to put his sheep on it for a few months, just to keep the grass, what there is of it, cut.
ANNIE	Did he now? That was generous of him.
THOMAS	I took him up on his offer since there was no sign of a proper tenant.
ANNIE	Well, don't be disappointed if you never get it set, now, sure you won't?
THOMAS	No, I won't.
ANNIE	How is the writing coming on?
THOMAS	I'd like to say I'm making progress but I fear I would be stretching the truth. It is very difficult.
ANNIE	Would I be right in saying, Thomas, that you came here to write but you didn't come here as a writer?
THOMAS	That would sum it up very well, Annie.

ANNIE	Ah, well, then it can be hard. You're only learning the trade, you might say.
THOMAS	You are very perceptive, Annie.
ANNIE	That goes with the job. Are you missing England?
THOMAS	I don't know. No, I'm not, really. I enjoy the company. Frances. Mary. They're refreshing after...well after... you know.
ANNIE	Thomas, you are the custodian of a great sadness.
THOMAS	What makes you think that?
ANNIE	We have an Irish saying 'Aithníonn ciaróg ámhain, ciaróg eile.'
THOMAS	What does it mean?
ANNIE	It takes one beetle to know another beetle.
THOMAS	Ah. You must walk the walk to talk the talk.
ANNIE	Yes, that would be the modern version.
THOMAS	Your husband?
ANNIE	Yes.
THOMAS	He was a good man?
ANNIE	He was.
THOMAS	Were you long married?
ANNIE	Three months. Ninety seven days, to be precise.
THOMAS	How did you meet him, Annie? Were you in Scotland?
ANNIE	No. He came over here the time they were setting up the local radio. He was a programme advisor. He just called in here one evening and that was how we met.
THOMAS	Love at first sight.
ANNIE	Hardly at our age. Love at first fright would be more like it. Funny we had this daftness for crosswords in common. The first thing I remember him doing was finishing the cryptic for me. I can still remember the clue 'is she a bit of a pest? Six letters. Rather. Do you get it? Rat, her. Isn't it funny, the daft things you remember?
THOMAS	I think that's lovely.
ANNIE	Do you? Anyway, he was a keen fisherman, too and there's plenty of that around here, so he was in here a lot. One thing led to another and we began going out together. It was great. It was very funny. You know

34

	the way Pat Grant keeps an eye on the bar if I have to go out anywhere. Well, Pat did nights for me when I'd go out with Colin. They used to call Pat 'Annie's babysitter.'
THOMAS	So, you married.
ANNIE	Yes. We did.
THOMAS	Tell me, a silly question but one I always ask. How did he propose?
ANNIE	Well there was nothing very romantic about it at all. Colin was a very practical man. We were sitting in the kitchen one night. He was on a six month contract and he says to me, 'Annie, my contract is up next month and I'll be going back to Scotland then unless there's something to keep me here. There's only one thing to keep me here and that's if you marry me.'
THOMAS	You're quite correct, Annie. It was more practical than romantic.
ANNIE	Arrah, what did we want romance for at our age.
THOMAS	But you loved him?
ANNIE	Loved him? The word love wouldn't do justice to what I thought about Colin. I adored the ground he walked on. Ah, I wish you had known him, Thomas. He was the kindest, calmest creature on God's earth. I remember thinking to myself one night that I didn't deserve a blessing like this at that stage of my life and within a month, God agreed and took him home.
THOMAS	Home?
ANNIE	To heaven.
THOMAS	I know there was an accident but I don't know the details. One doesn't wish to pry.
ANNIE	Prying wouldn't be noticed around here. There's no secret. They went fishing one day. Colin, Pat Grant and James Quinn. I warned them that the boat hadn't been used for a few years but Colin said he had checked it and it seemed alright. They went out on the lake and a panel that was tarred on the side came off and the boat capsized with water and they were all pitched into the lake. Quinn was the only middling swimmer. He got

	Pat Grant onto the top of the overturned boat but when he went looking for Colin he was gone. The divers got him the following day.
THOMAS	Oh, God, it must have been awful for you?
ANNIE	Ah, now, can you imagine, poor Pat having to face in here to tell me? And do you know what the worst of the whole thing was?
THOMAS	What?
ANNIE	Canon O'Donnell that was Parish Priest here at the time asked me would he be buried here or in Scotland, as he put it, 'with his own people.'
THOMAS	Oh, dear.
ANNIE	That hurt. Do you know, Thomas, some of these clergymen are sent by God to test us.
THOMAS	Indeed. I presume Colin was buried here 'with his own people.'
ANNIE	He was. I go and talk to him for a few minutes every day.
THOMAS	Are you bitter?
ANNIE	With who?
THOMAS	God.
ANNIE	Much point in that. If it came to a fight, God has a bigger army than I have. And anyway, what would I be bitter about. Didn't he give me Colin in the first place?
THOMAS	Yes, but to snatch him away like that…
ANNIE	*(interrupting)* You miss the point, Thomas. All the memories I have are beautiful. Colin was taken before I could see any faults in him. Isn't that lovely? I knew a perfect man. I'll bet you there's not many women can say that? Hah?
THOMAS	It is a remarkable story told by a remarkable lady.
ANNIE	Well, you know, of course, Thomas, why I told you all that?
THOMAS	Why?
ANNIE	Pat Grant told me one night, partly because he was drunk and partly because he needed to tell me. When the accident happened, Colin was nearest the upturned boat but James Quinn swam past him to get to Pat

Grant. Quinn says it was because he thought Colin could swim but it wasn't. He didn't do it on purpose or anything. It's just nature. He did it because we look after our own first. Don't forget that, Thomas. No matter how long you are here or how well you think you are settled, if there's a problem you'll be the last to be saved.

THOMAS Yes. I see.

ANNIE So, if you heard a shot going across your bows tonight, pay heed to it because you can be sure that everyone else heard it as well.

SLOW FADE

SCENE SIX

The Dolan kitchen. Early evening. Frances at the table, studying.
Mary enters.

MARY	I see Thomas coming up the lane.
FRANCES	Oh, good. He must have read the essay.
MARY	He has the copy book with him, anyway.
FRANCES	I hope he liked it.
MARY	He's a great help to you, Frances.
FRANCES	Yeah, it's a big change to have someone around the place with a bit of intelligence.
MARY	Thanks very much.
FRANCES	Ah, you know what I mean.
MARY	Yes, I suppose I do. But not everyone would and you should think before you say things like that.
	Thomas enters.
THOMAS	Good evening.
MARY	Good evening, Thomas. How are you?
THOMAS	Fine, Mary. This is good, Frances. Very good.
FRANCES	Do you think?
MARY	Is it not a bit long, Thomas? Would she have time to write a composition that length in an examination?
FRANCES	An essay, Mam.
MARY	We did compositions when I was going to school.
THOMAS	And a composition is an excellent name for it, Mary. *(sitting)* You see, Frances, you are trying to compose, to communicate ideas and never forget the three rules of communication.
FRANCES	Which are?
THOMAS	Tell them what you are going to tell them, tell them what you want to tell them and tell them what you've told them.
FRANCES	What?

38

THOMAS	Well, look. It's like the news on Radio or Television. It starts with the headlines, that's what they're going to tell you, then the main body of the news, that's what they want to tell you and it finishes with a recap of the headlines, which is what they have told you.
MARY	I never knew that. It makes sense when it's explained.
THOMAS	Yes and these three rules hold good for any form of communication. When…anyone preaches a sermon, for instance or makes a speech, they use these rules.
FRANCES	And I should use them in my essay or composition?
THOMAS	Well, bear them in mind for a structure. When an examiner sees the structure he will feel he is dealing with someone who knows what they are doing.
	Frances laughs.
MARY	What's so funny?
FRANCES	Well, I was just thinking, I must explain this to Dad. He's always asking 'why have I to tell you everything three times?' Now, I'll tell him 'it's the law of communication, Da.' That'll shake him.
MARY	Why can't you leave your father alone for five minutes and stop picking at him?
FRANCES	Arrah, mother, I'm only messing, sure I love him to bits.
MARY	You do.
FRANCES	Well, I love him in bits.
THOMAS	Well, I must away. Good luck, tomorrow. You'll call in on your way home and let me know how Biology went?
FRANCES	Have the kettle on.
THOMAS	Definitely.
MARY	Thomas, thanks for all your help with Frances. I don't know what she'd have done without you. Myself and her father aren't much good to her with her lessons.
FRANCES	Lessons, Mother. Lessons went out with the Ark. You sound ancient.
MARY	That's because I am. At least I feel ancient. Anyway, thank you, Thomas.
THOMAS	Not at all. It has been a pleasure. Frances is extremely bright. Very invigorating.

FRANCES	And Thomas, you are a genius.
THOMAS	Oh, dear, don't let Pat Grant hear you say that. I'd be afraid he'd find some use for me.
	They laugh as Paul enters.
PAUL	That must have been a good joke?
THOMAS	Oh, hello, Paul. No, it wasn't a joke, more an observation.
PAUL	An observation?
THOMAS	About Pat Grant.
PAUL	The same Pat is no joke.
THOMAS	Oh, I know that.
PAUL	The widow below has the best joke.
MARY	What's that?
PAUL	She has Pat Grant, Thomas and Colin. Paddy the Irishman, Paddy the Englishman and Paddy the Scotsman.
FRANCES	Dad, that's horrible. That's not funny. That's typical.
PAUL	What is?
FRANCES	If you don't understand something, mock it.
PAUL	And what do I not understand now, genius?
FRANCES	Will I make out a list for you?
MARY	Stop it. Are you going to town or not?
PAUL	I'm ready if she is.
THOMAS	Big day tomorrow, Paul. For Frances.
PAUL	For us all, Thomas. The start of the finish, isn't it?
THOMAS	Well the start of phase two anyway. Biology.
PAUL	Yes. Biology. The study of living organisms.
FRANCES	God, Da, you're coming on. You've been in the dictionary again.
PAUL	Come on. We'll be late.
MARY	Will you be back at six?
PAUL	We will. Sure all we have to do is call to the chipper for her job and straight home.
FRANCES	You're forgetting. If he doesn't up the rate, I'm not taking the job.
MARY	Don't turn it down. You won't get anything else.
FRANCES	Ah, sure maybe Thomas will give me a job for the summer, putting paper in his typewriter or sharpening

	his pencils.
THOMAS	*(laughing)*
	I'm afraid that the rate of pay would not be very attractive.
FRANCES	Oh yeah, but the job satisfaction. The company would be super.
PAUL	Come on.
FRANCES	That's only twice, Da. You have to tell me three times. It's the law of communication.
PAUL	What?
FRANCES	You wouldn't understand. Come on.
	They exit.
THOMAS	She's a lovely girl, Mary. You're very fortunate.
MARY	We would be, if we weren't losing her.
THOMAS	But that's the way of the world, Mary. Children must move on, leave the nest.
MARY	Ah, I know that. It's just that we never prepared for it. Isn't that daft? We've known she'd leave for the last eighteen years and yet we never prepared ourselves for it. I don't know what Paul will do when she goes.
THOMAS	Paul? But surely there'll be peace in the valley, as the song says. I mean, anytime I see them together they are disagreeing about something.
MARY	That's because they're too alike. And because he loves her too much.
THOMAS	Yes?
MARY	Since the first day he held her, he has lived for that child. She never leaves his mind. It's like an obsession.
THOMAS	Yes?
MARY	Yes. Oh, I suppose it's great in ways. It gives him something to work for. To strive for. Only that everyone else can feel a bit left out. Excluded.
THOMAS	Everyone else? Who is there only you, Mary.
MARY	I remember being at the mart with him one day. I can't even remember what I was doing there. He got a wee bit more than he expected for a few cattle and he was like a child on Christmas morning. I worked out what he got and I sez 'I don't know what you're getting

	excited about; it's only about an extra tenner.' But he says, 'I'll be able to buy a couple of Prize Bonds for Frances' everything had to be shared with Frances.
THOMAS	Does she know this? That he feels such love for her?
MARY	Arrah, Thomas, she's young. A teenager. When you're a teenager anyone over twenty one is the walking dead. She hasn't time for anyone that isn't on the same wavelength as herself. Anyone who doesn't believe in the same things, who doesn't not believe in the same things. She'll know it in time. I hope she knows it before it's too late.
THOMAS	Does he ever tell her he loves her?
MARY	How do you mean? She's his daughter.
THOMAS	I know that. But does he ever actually say it to her?
MARY	Fellas like Paul don't tell you they love you. They show you. And if you're not looking you won't see it.
THOMAS	But you are looking, Mary?
MARY	Some of the time, Thomas, some of the time. Sometimes you have to look very hard.
	Pause
	Anyway, I'd better see what the hens left us today.
THOMAS	And I must return to my work.
MARY	How is it going?
THOMAS	Don't ask. One step forward, two steps back.
	(as they exit)
MARY	I'd love to be able to do something like that. You know. To write. I'd love to be able to do that.
THOMAS	So would I, Mary. So would I.

FADE

SCENE SEVEN

Bar. Annie and Pat doing crossword.

PAT	Isn't that a hoor. It's always the easy ones that stump you.
ANNIE	It'll come. Don't worry.
PAT	It better or there'll be no sleep the night.
ANNIE	Well, you won't get much in the morning. They're starting a road in at Humpties.
PAT	Who?
ANNIE	The Forestry. They were in here today. Said the machinery would be going up in the morning. They wanted me to know so that I wouldn't be alarmed by the noise.
PAT	Well, Jaysus, that's typical. They wouldn't put a road in it when there was people living in it and now they'll do the devil and all when they want to plant trees.
ANNIE	Had Humpty no road?
PAT	Not at all. Hadn't they to cross three stiles and two seochs to get to the road. Do you not mind the craic the time young Humpty was getting the Confirmation?
ANNIE	No. What was that?
PAT	Arrah, you do. 'Twas the time that Confirmation was only every four years and there used to be a fierce hullabaloo in case fellas wouldn't pass the exam because you'd be put back four years. Anyways, Young Humpty was always missing from school. Mandrake, Sergeant Healy called him because he disappeared so often and he was nearly fourteen when he came for Confirmation and didn't the Canon fail him. The mother, Mrs. Humpty, was in an awful state because he'd be eighteen when he'd get another chance and they'd be the talk of the country so she took off across the three stiles and two seochs and made for the presbytery to see the Canon. 'I can't let him go on,' sez the Canon, 'I asked him a simple question of faith and

43

he was unable to answer.' 'What did you ask him?' says yer wan. 'I asked him which one of the three divine persons died.' 'Arrah, Canon, sez she, 'sure we're living so far in off the road, the whole three of them could be dead and we wouldn't hear a word about it.'

ANNIE   *(laughing)*
              Oh, I remember it now. But sure that wasn't true at all.

PAT   It could be true and never to happen. And now they'll put a road in it.

              Paul and Thomas enter.

PAT   A number of fingers

THOMAS   Sorry?

PAT   A number of fingers. Five letters. O is the middle one.

PAUL   Forty.

PAT   What?

PAUL   Forty fingers.

PAT   What kind of a gobshite are you? Forty fingers. Anyway O is the middle letter.

THOMAS   A whiskey and a beer Annie, please. Pat?

PAT   Half one.

THOMAS   And another whiskey.

ANNIE   How is the exam going, Paul?

PAUL   Alright, I think. She's not saying much, for a change.

ANNIE   What is she saying to you, Thomas?

THOMAS   Maths was a little difficult. But not her fault. I gather the Maths teacher would be weak enough.

PAT   A bad tradesman always blames the tools.

ANNIE   If I know Frances, she'll get her points.

THOMAS   I have no doubt she will.

PAUL   And that, I suppose, will be the last we'll see of her, except for an odd week-end and at Christmas.

ANNIE   Won't she have to come back to defend Pat when the bank takes him to court.

THOMAS   I doubt that. I'd imagine Frances would be only interested in cases she could win.

PAUL   Yahoo! That tightened you up, Pat.

PAT   Smart boy wanted. Not too smart.

THOMAS   Sorry?

PAT	That was a sign in McDonagh's shop window one time. Smart boy wanted, not too smart. Did you get the land set yet?
THOMAS	No. I fear it is impossible.
PAT	Well, is it? I'd have thought Paul having the sheep grazing it would be a great advertisement for it.
THOMAS	Yes?
PAT	You'd have thought the whole country would want it when they saw it was so useful.
PAUL	You'd want to have another look at that sign in McDonagh's shop window
PAT	Why don't you plant it?
PAUL	Why would he do that?
PAT	Look at the grants. You'd plant it for the size of the grant and you'd get a headage payment every year.
THOMAS	Really? How much would it be?
PAT	I'm not sure. I'd have to look it up.
THOMAS	I didn't know about that. Did you. Paul?
PAUL	You have to think of your neighbours if you're going planting ground. Them auld trees put acids into the soil and it spills into the fields around them.
ANNIE	Still, there's a lot of trees being planted.
PAUL	Them's not trees they're planting. They're headstones. This place will finish up a cemetery full of trees before they're finished. If the land was lying up against Pat he wouldn't be as keen to plant it for you.
PAT	Indeed you could fire ahead, as long as I got a Christmas tree off it.
PAUL	What would you be doing with a Christmas tree? You won't have anyone to look at it.
PAT	I'll have as many as you the year.
ANNIE	Aisy, lads. Talking about timber, Thomas, did you get Tom Sawyer that time?
THOMAS	Tom Sawyer?
PAUL	Patsy Layden. The carpenter.
THOMAS	Oh, yes. I did. He's with me at the moment. Doing excellent work.
PAT	Talented man, Patsy.

THOMAS	Very quiet. Hardly a word out of him.
PAT	That goes with his trade.
THOMAS	Yes?
PAT	Yeah. When you think about it, Joseph the Carpenter must have been the quietest man ever. A pure saint if there ever was one. Hammering away making chairs, tables and whatever and I suppose not getting paid for half of it and the wife arrives in and tells him she's expecting and she won't tell him who the father is 'cause he knows it's not his. She says it's the Son of God and he's expected to swallow that. Then the young buck turns out pure useless, won't even sweep the sawdust off the floor for him only preaching and teaching and up to all sorts of tricks with water.
ANNIE	Stop, Pat.
PAT	Next think is he arrives back to the house with twelve latchicos slinging out of him and the mother is expected to put up grub for all. And still there's no record anywhere of poor auld Joe ever saying boo to a goose. So now, is it any wonder that carpenters are quiet men?
THOMAS	The Vatican should be informed about you.
PAUL	I think Pat is on the Canon's hit list this years.
THOMAS	I'm thinking of buying the car from Patsy.
ANNIE	The car?
PAUL	The Hillman?
THOMAS	Yes. I will have to go to Dublin fairly regularly and it seems a waste using public transport. The price seems quite reasonable.
PAUL	I'm sure it is. *(to Pat)* Good man, Patsy.
THOMAS	Yes and he says he has a tow bar and he will put it on for free.
PAT	Good man, aris. Is he putting the tow bar on the front or the back?
THOMAS	Sorry?
PAT	Nothing. Well if you're bringing it to Dublin be sure

	you don't wash it 'till you get back.
THOMAS	Why?
PAT	Any auld dirt or clay you pick up in Dublin bring it back with you. Any extra bit of land helps round here.
ANNIE	Don't heed these playboys, Thomas. You have a good fruit garden up there.
THOMAS	Excellent. All sorts. I must bring you down some gooseberries later.
ANNIE	Oh do. That'd be great. I'll make a tart for you.
PAUL	You won't have much left when the birds are finished with them. The Callaghans always put out scarecrows. Are they not in the shed?
THOMAS	Yes. I've seen them there.
PAT	And why don't you put them out?
THOMAS	I leave more value upon having birds in my garden than fruit. I give them my fruit, they give me their song.
PAUL	Begod, I know what I'd give them. The two barrels.
ANNIE	Still, it's a nice thought. You can tell the fellas in Brussels that, Pat.
PAT	They'd need to be told something. Were you in the mart the day, Paul?
PAUL	I was. For a half hour. 'Twould put you off. I left it.
PAT	I never seen things so bad.
THOMAS	In farming?
PAT	No, in ice hockey. What the hell do you think we're talking about? I don't know how we're going to keep going.
PAUL	We're banjaxed.
PAT	We would be if we weren't too thick to cave in. Do you know, I saw a beast today going the very same money as four years ago.
PAUL	I wouldn't doubt it.
PAT	And I worked out that the feedstuff is costing nearly two and a half times what it was four years ago.
THOMAS	But what about all the grants you get from Brussels, Pat?
PAT	Look, Clever Dick, if you were sitting on your own in my house every night you'd know I gave Brussels far

	more that it ever gave me.
PAUL	But, sure, Thomas you'd have the answers for us, wouldn't you? Haven't you all the answers for us?
THOMAS	I must say that if I were in your position there would appear to me to be only one solution.
PAT	What's that?
THOMAS	Declare war on America.
ANNIE	Ah, Jay, that's a good one.
PAUL	Didn't I tell you he'd have all the answers.
PAT	I think, Thomas, Callaghan's place is getting to you at last. You're listening too much to the birds. You have them on the brain.
THOMAS	No, look at the logic behind the argument. Declare war on America. Send a unit off to bomb Boston, making sure, obviously, that the Americans knew who they were and that they were coming. The Americans could capture them and then, in turn, they would drop a bomb on some vacant bog-land in the West of Ireland. At that point, you surrender.
PAUL	Surrender?
ANNIE	Surrender?
THOMAS	Yes. History indicates what happens next. Look at Germany. Look at Japan. After they surrendered to America, the United States poured billions of dollars into the re-development of those countries. Look at them today. I tell you, you wouldn't recognise the place in five years time.

There is a pause whilst Pat and Paul consider the suggestion.

Finally.

PAT	Aren't you forgetting one thing?
THOMAS	What?
PAT	Supposing we won and they surrendered?
THOMAS	How could that possibly happen?
PAUL	You see. The English always underestimate the Irish.

Paul and Pat laugh.

PAT	Drinks?
PAUL	No. I have the car and they might be out. Have one

	you, Thomas, if you like.
THOMAS	No, I'm fine. I'll go with you.
ANNIE	God, Thomas, that was a great invention. War on America.
	She exits.
PAT	Oh, but the English are great inventors. Soccer, Rugby, Cricket. They invented all them. And then they had to invent Scotland and Wales so that at least they'd have someone they'd be able to beat playing them.
THOMAS	Touché. Well done, Pat.
PAUL	Come on. We'll go. Goodnight.
PAT	Safe home.
	Paul and Thomas exit.
	Thomas turns at door and addresses Pat.
THOMAS	Frost.
PAT	What?
THOMAS	A number of fingers. Frost.
	He exits. Pat looks after him, then goes to the table and looks at the crossword.
PAT	*(to himself)*
	Well fuck you.
	He goes to the door and speaks out.
	And if you have any friends in America, fuck them too.

FADE

END OF ACT ONE

INTERVAL

ACT TWO

SCENE EIGHT

Dolan's kitchen. Paul and Mary

PAUL	Well she'd better take the job this time. I'm not going down with her again.
MARY	Sure, she will take it, Paul. Isn't she getting what she wants?
PAUL	She doesn't know that.
MARY	Well, why would he have sent for her the second time so?
PAUL	I don't know. Maybe he has cards to give her or something. It's that buck below in Callaghan's place that has her this way. Bloody communist.
MARY	Communist?
PAUL	Aye. Going around with an answer for everything. Jesus, if he knew anything he'd hardly be stuck below in that place feeding the birds with blackcurrants.
MARY	Well, he was a big help to Frances.
PAUL	He was. Why? What's in it for him? By Christ, if he lays a finger on that girl the Guards'll be gathering up bits of him for the next ten years.
MARY	Ah, for God's sake, Thomas wouldn't touch Frances. He's not like that.
PAUL	How do you know?
MARY	I know. He's just a nice gentleman that wants to help his neighbours.
PAUL	Aye. Well no one does anything for nothing. No one ever gave us anything for nothing. Nor why should they? I wouldn't expect it.
MARY	Well, maybe then you should give him the price of the setting of the land.

PAUL	What land?
MARY	Where you put the sheep.
PAUL	What? Amn't I only doing him a favour. Keeping the grass down.
MARY	Well, sure you said yourself; no one does anything for nothing. I don't see the sheep spitting out the grass after they eat it.
PAUL	Now, lookit, don't be trying to be smart, you.
	Frances enters.
	Oh, here's another smart one landed. It wasn't off the ground you licked the smartness.
FRANCES	Well, I hope you weren't suggesting that I got any off you.
MARY	*(quickly)*
	How did the exams go?
FRANCES	Great. Didn't the poem come up that Thomas worked on with me and I got a great essay. It was wide open for using the three rules.
PAUL	What three rules?
FRANCES	Never mind. You wouldn't understand. Anyway, I called to Thomas there now. He's picking a bowl of gooseberries to bring up to you later.
PAUL	It's a sight he has any left with the birds.
FRANCES	I never saw as much fruit down there. Thomas says that in life the more you give away the more you get back. God, when I think of the Callaghans, they'd nearly be out writing numbers on the blackcurrants in case they lost one.
PAUL	You knew where you stood with the Callaghans.
FRANCES	You did. That was a big help to you.
PAUL	Oh and I suppose you'd prefer the stranger man. The man from God knows where, running from God knows what. Lookit, Frances, I'm not happy with you being down there on your own with that fella.
FRANCES	What are you saying?
MARY	Ah, your father is just afraid, Frances. Thomas is lovely but we know nothing about him.
FRANCES	Oh, aye and we knew about the Callaghans. They were

51

	alright, were they? Pair of perverts. Every time I went into them, leering at me and trying to look up under my skirt. But they were the good neighbours.
PAUL	What are you saying?
FRANCES	What am I saying about what?
PAUL	About them looking at you?
FRANCES	Nothing.
	(to Mary)
	I'd go in at five o'clock on my way home from school and do you know what the pair would be at? Sitting, drooling in front of the television looking at Rikki Lake. For God's sake. Can you imagine?
	(quoting)
	"I married a monkey and he's being unfaithful to me with my dog."
PAUL	What are you saying about them looking at you?
MARY	Leave it, Paul. Don't heed it.
PAUL	By God, that pair is lucky they're dead.
FRANCES	Why?
PAUL	Looking at a daughter of mine like that.
FRANCES	Arrah, will you cop on to yourself. Isn't that what keeps auld fellas alive, looking at young ones. If they weren't looking I'd be worried. Anyway, are you bringing me down to see this Shylock?
MARY	Your father says to take the job this time.
FRANCES	I will, if he bends on the money.
PAUL	Well, you won't get what you're looking for.
FRANCES	No, but I'll get what I want. Come on.
	She exits.
PAUL	Jesus, you can never get the better of that one.
MARY	Will you go with her and don't put the car over the ditch arguing with her. If you can't get the better of her will you stop trying to?
PAUL	Oh God give me patience.
	He goes. Mary takes school bag and puts it on table. She takes out examination paper and begins to study it. Thomas enters bearing bowl of gooseberries.
THOMAS	Mary, I brought you a bowl of gooseberries.

MARY	Oh, thanks, Thomas.
THOMAS	You might like to make a pie. I don't think there's enough for jam.
MARY	I'll make a tart with them.
THOMAS	Yes, that would be nice.
MARY	Sit down. I was just going to make a cup of tea. You'll have one?
THOMAS	Thank you. I will. You're studying, I see.
MARY	Studying, how are you. It's double Dutch to me. I might as well be at the crossword with Annie.
THOMAS	As Geography papers go, I think it was quite reasonable. Frances was happy enough with the English paper, as well, I think.
MARY	Yes. She said. Geography. Lovely word that. 'Study of the Earth's physical features, climate and population.'
THOMAS	Yes.
MARY	That's what the dictionary says. I remember when I was at the National School, the Cigire came. Oh, that's the Irish for Inspector, Thomas.
THOMAS	Oh, I see.
MARY	Anyway, he came to the school one day and I heard himself and The Master talking and the Cigire was saying that he always found that the girls were better than the boys at geography and the Master said it was because the girls had travel in their heads and were dreaming of far away places and were interested in learning about those places
THOMAS	An interesting theory. Yes, could be.
MARY	I liked Geography. For all the good it done me. I never got to see further than Castlebar the day of a football match or a day at the Galway races.
THOMAS	You didn't go to second level, secondary school, Mary?
MARY	No. I was lucky to get finishing first level. In those days you didn't have any great notions. I finished Primary School and went working in McDonagh's shop and the only bit of geography I saw after that was a map of Ireland on the back of the exercise book that you wrote the slate into.

THOMAS	You would have liked more education?
MARY	Oh, I would. I'd like to win the Lotto today but I have the same chance. It was different times. No one encouraged you to go above your station.
THOMAS	When did you meet Paul?
MARY	Arrah, I know Paul all my life. We were in school together. We started going out when we were about twenty and we married five or six years later.
THOMAS	You got a good man, Mary.
MARY	Yes, I did. But I didn't want a good man, Thomas. I wanted a great man. I wanted a man like you, Thomas. A man whose imagination didn't come to an end at the last ditch of his land. A man that would take risks in life, go for a big thing. What did I get? A copy of his father. Big, strong, safe. Worst of all, safe.
THOMAS	Safe?
MARY	A man that didn't want to be a success. Just wanted not to be a failure.
THOMAS	Ah, but Mary, you've had a good life. You love Paul. You love each other.
MARY	Love? *(quoting)* 'The noun. Warm affection. Sexual passion. Wholehearted passion for something. The verb. To have a great affection for: feel sexual passion for; enjoy very much.' See, I even had to look up that word to see what it meant. And do you know what I discovered, Thomas, when I was looking it up?
THOMAS	What?
MARY	That in tennis the word love means a score of nothing. Now I thought that was nearer the mark.
THOMAS	That's a wonderful thing about the people here.
MARY	What?
THOMAS	The openness. Nobody in England would ever say what you've just said. The English are so reserved. There's a serious contradiction about them. At night, when they put the lights on, they leave their curtains open and yet they resent anyone looking into their houses, into their

	lives. Here, it's the opposite.
MARY	I wouldn't be so sure about that.
THOMAS	Here, people talk so much.
MARY	And say so little.
THOMAS	Yes?
MARY	Yeah. If you listen, in Annie's for instance, on a busy night, everyone is talking but nobody is saying anything. Anything important.
THOMAS	Maybe not, but at least they're talking.
MARY	Silence might be better than pretending.

Pause

	Thomas, are you very lonely?
THOMAS	Not now. No. Not since I came here.
MARY	Here?
THOMAS	Yes. Mary, my work in England was very intense, very focused. I didn't have time or space for friendships, relationships. Here has been a wonderful release.
MARY	Will you stay?
THOMAS	As long as I can. Yes. Why?
MARY	Maybe it'll be less lonely then.
THOMAS	For you?
MARY	Yes.
THOMAS	But how can you be lonely? You have Paul, Frances, neighbours. How can you be lonely?
MARY	Is that what it's about? Life? Is this all there is to it?
THOMAS	What bothers you, Mary?

Pause

MARY	I feel so...so unfulfilled. So empty. When I think of all I denied myself. All the risks I could have taken, should have taken.
THOMAS	Risks?
MARY	Yes. Why can't I go and buy a cottage in England?
THOMAS	You think what I'm doing is taking risks?
MARY	When I was in school we were brought for a day out to Rosses Point. It's a beautiful place, Thomas, with a lovely, long, golden beach. I wanted to walk the length of the beach but the tide was in. While the rest were playing in the sand-hills I set off through the water.

THOMAS	Why?
MARY	I didn't want to wait for the tide to go out to walk the beach. I wanted to do something, anything, before anyone else. Of course, I was brought back, slapped for being bold and told to wait for everyone else. What would anyone ever have achieved if they waited for everyone else? But that's what my life has been. Waiting for the crowd. I'd just like to leave something behind. A trace of having been here. A mark in the sand.
THOMAS	But, Mary, Frances is your monument. Your imprint on the world.
MARY	I never was anything. Never did anything. I'd love to see Chelmsford. I looked for it in Frances' atlas. It's in Essex, isn't it?
THOMAS	Yes, but believe me, Mary, you would be disappointed.
MARY	No. I know what disappointed is. No need to look that one up in the dictionary. When we did Geography in school, I was fascinated by Madagascar.
THOMAS	Madagascar?
MARY	Yes. Have you ever been to Madagascar, Thomas?
THOMAS	Yes. It's beautiful. You would not be disappointed with Madagascar.
MARY	I knew that. Oh, I'd love if someone would come and sweep me off my feet. Take me to Madagascar. I'd like a different definition of love. Out of a different dictionary.
THOMAS	Well, that can happen yet.
MARY	Some chance. Are you going to run away with me, Thomas?
THOMAS	Now, Mary, we both know that's not possible.
MARY	Oh, it's possible, Thomas. It's just not going to happen, is it?
THOMAS	No.
	Pause
	Your life is not a disappointment, Mary. You know that. It has been worth it, hasn't it?
MARY	Has it?
THOMAS	Frances?

MARY	Ah, yes, Frances. Yes, it has been worth it. I suppose. But you wouldn't know this because you wouldn't be looking for it but Frances is a very selfish girl.
THOMAS	Focused, yes.
MARY	Is that the nice name for it? For selfish? She was always that way. When she was born she brought my insides with her in case there'd be anyone else. Now, she has us bled dry of love she's off out into the world and the two of us have to face each other at last without her to deflect us, come between us, bind us. Now we'll find out all about love or if such a thing exists.
THOMAS	But is that not the way with all children? They grow up. Parents lose them.
MARY	Of course it is. I'm not blaming the child. I suppose I'm just resenting the fact that she's doing what I wanted to do, what I was never offered.
THOMAS	You know, Mary, you should be very proud of what you have achieved with Frances.
MARY	We are. But Paul is very jealous about Frances. He has too much love for her.
THOMAS	As any father should.
MARY	It's just that she's very close to you, Thomas. Paul is finding that hard, especially with her going. He's looking for something or someone to blame. Try to make sure it's not you.
THOMAS	How do you mean? Surely he doesn't think…
MARY	*(interrupting)* Frances compares him to you and he comes out badly.
THOMAS	But why? I have never achieved anything. Paul is twice the man I can ever be. Why should she think otherwise?
MARY	Frances is young. She thinks love without complication is possible. I know it's not. **Pause**
THOMAS	What do you want from the rest of your life?
MARY	You don't want to know that, Thomas. You don't want to know that. **Pause**

	Could you make a promise to me, Thomas?
THOMAS	Certainly. I hope so.
MARY	If you leave here, don't bring Frances with you.
THOMAS	I can safely promise that. . It would fly in the face of everything I believe in. That I hold to be true.
MARY	So you won't take Frances from us.
THOMAS	No. I promise. Mary, I'm sorry if I can't give you what you are looking for.
MARY	No, Thomas, you can't. But I got what I wanted.
THOMAS	I feel I cheated a little.
MARY	In what way?
THOMAS	Well, it was easy to promise not to bring Frances, She'll be going anyway.
MARY	Yes, but there's a difference between going and being taken.
	Pause
THOMAS	You'll be alright, Mary?
MARY	Oh God, I'll be alright, Thomas. I'm always alright. It would be nice, just once, to be a little better than that

FADE

58

SCENE NINE

Annie's bar. Pat is positioned behind the bar doing a crossword. Paul enters.

PAUL   Are you the boss the day, Pat?

PAT   I'm the boss when the boss is away. Annie is gone to the grave and she said she'd get her hair done after that.

PAUL   So you're babysitting.

PAT   I'm babysitting. God, do you remember, Paul. Poor auld Colin. What?

PAUL   We don't seem to have much luck with foreign visitors here. Give me a half one.

PAT   Be God, this time of the day? Celebrating something?

PAUL   'Tis the last day of the Leaving. Will you have one?

PAT   No, Paul. Not when I'm this side of the counter. It wouldn't be fair on Annie.

PAUL   Sound man, so.

PAT   How did the exams go?

PAUL   Well, I don't know about the day but it seems to be alright up to now. But sure how would I know? If you want a full report you'd need to ask Mr. Hopkinson.

PAT   Oh?

PAUL   What do you make of that fella, Pat?

PAT   Well now, I'll tell you
        Pause
        He's the kind of a fella that you wouldn't know what kind of a fella he is.

PAUL   Jesus, you're as bad as he is. Will you talk English?

PAT   That'd be a fair thing to say to the Englishman, 'will you talk English'?

PAUL   Ah, you know what I mean.

PAT   Indeed, I do. What do you make of him? You have him beside you.

PAUL   I don't know. He's a good enough sort of a gent. But there's something not right about him. Arrah, I

59

suppose, in some ways, he's as awkward as a turkey in a stubble field but that's because he's not in his own place. Mary says he was a big help to Frances and maybe he was. But why? Hah? What's in it for him? I see him looking at her and I don't like the way he looks at her.

PAT   What do you mean? What other way would he look at her? Isn't she a fine young girl?

PAUL   What the hell are you saying?

PAT   Arrah, Jesus, Paul, can't you be proud of the girl. You don't own her. Never did. Never will.

PAUL   It's alright for you.

PAT   How would it be alright for me? Do you think I was never through it with our lassie? Who had to go after young Donoghue with a hedge knife? Hah?

PAUL   Give me another half one.
        Pause
        I just didn't think I'd ever see this day. Myself and Frances fought like dogs for the last eighteen years and do you know, I'd walk across a floor of rusty razor blades in my bare feet for her. I was bringing her down the day to sort out the job for the summer and she says 'well that's the Leaving over, thank God' and I just thought to myself, that's the leaving started.

PAT   Can I give you a bit of advice, Paul?

PAUL   What?

PAT   Don't take this the wrong way now. And if you get on your high horse I'll shut up. But I can only tell you my story, not yours. Let the daughter go. Leave her off. She'll make her way. You'll have to accept that she'll go out into the world. Meet fellas. Date fellas. Maybe even go to bed with a fella.

PAUL   Shut up.

PAT   Christ, if you're ever charged with having patience I'll appear for the defence. Will you listen? You need to know this. And remember it. She'll meet fellas and she'll arrive home to you sometime with a fella and she'll say she's going to marry him and let him be

60

	black, white or the colour of the county jersey and whether you like him or hate him, say nothing because you are not her proprietor.
PAUL	Aisy said.
PAT	Aisy said. But this much more I'll tell you. Let your daughter go and you'll keep your wife.
PAUL	My wife?
PAT	Yes. Don't take your eye off the ball. That's what happened me.
PAUL	How do you mean?
PAT	Look, you had Mary before you had Frances and you'll have her after. Don't let her think you think more of her daughter than you do of her. Don't devalue Mary.
PAUL	Arrah, Pat, you're talking shite. Mary is my wife.
PAT	And Rita is mine. But that don't count. What do I see of her now? Hah? All we concerned ourselves with was rearing children. Putting grub on the table, clothes on their back and books in their schoolbags. We'd be too tired to fart in the evenings. Falling asleep each side of the fire. Jaysus, I don't know did we have one conversation about ourselves in twenty years. And when they were gone, what was left? Two strangers sharing a house. And now we visit each other like it's a duty or something. Don't let that happen to you. Study your case now or you'll find yourself falling asleep at night doing what lonely men must do to stay sane.
	Pause
PAUL	Arrah, you don't know what you're talking about. Give me another half one.
PAT	Have you the car?
PAUL	I have. I'll be alright. She's on the back road.
PAT	You know, you're lucky. That one knows what she wants to do. What she wants to achieve in life. She has spirit. She'll be something great yet.
PAUL	Oh aye, President of Ireland.
PAT	Don't mock it. President Frances Dolan. It has a ring to it.
PAUL	What will become of us, Pat?

PAT	No big surprise there. What will become of us? Here? In this place? Are you not watching it for the last twenty years? Hah? We're all in the same boat and if you lean out and look at the side of it you'll see that the name is Titanic. And Paul, you, me and Annie are the three fiddlers in the band playing Nearer my God to Thee and she's sinking fast and our children are going off in the lifeboats. But we won't go, for we're too thick and if we're rescued we'll be called fools and if we go down we'll be heroes. Dead heroes. So take your pick, me boy, but know two things. Your daughter is gone on the lifeboat and your wife will go on one too if you don't persuade her to stay and play the drums with you.
PAUL	Do you think it's like that, Pat? Do you think I'll end up like you?
PAT	I don't know but there's no point in one man making a mistake if another man don't learn from it. That's all I'm saying. We mightn't all start off the same way around here but if we don't watch it we'll all finish up the same way.
PAUL	I'll go down and collect Frances.
PAT	Where is she?
PAUL	There's a party down in the hotel. For the Leaving. I suppose they're on the beer.
PAT	Is she drinking any of yours?
PAUL	No.
PAT	Well then, shut up. Remember the lease on her is up. And anyway, there's too much song and dance about these Leaving students drinking. I was below in the hotel last year when they were in it. I was watching the whole performance. Bejaysus, I drank more at my confirmation. Will you be back?
PAUL	No. I'll go home. I'll be down the night.
PAT	Do. And lookit, bring Mary down with you. We don't see enough of her and it's a good night to bring her out. We might have a game of twenty five.
PAUL	Aye. Right so. Right. I'll do that.

PAT	Bring the Englishman. We'll show him how to play.
PAUL	No, Pat, do you know, tonight, I think I'll leave him where he is.
PAT	Right so. Sound. See you.
PAUL	See you.

Paul exits. Pat returns to crossword as lights cross fade to Thomas' kitchen. Thomas is leaning over typewriter, reading typed material. He is smoking. Frances enters carrying schoolbag.

SCENE TEN

FRANCES   Oh, smoking, Thomas. You'll get cancer. Sr. Margaret used to say if God had meant us to smoke he'd have put a chimney on our heads.

THOMAS   I'm sorry that you caught me smoking, Frances. It's a little relief mechanism that I turn to when I'm under pressure.

FRANCES   And what pressure are you under, a gradh?

THOMAS   Oh nothing I can't handle. Anyway, your pressure is over.

FRANCES   For the moment. Oh, I got the job fixed up for the summer. Got him to jack up the wages. God, listening to my father you'd think that I should be glad to work for nothing.

THOMAS   So, university beckons.

FRANCES   I hope so. Yeah, I think so. I worked hard to get into college, Thomas.

THOMAS   Now, when you get there, don't forget that you have to work hard to get out of college as well.

FRANCES   Well, aren't you the clever boy now. That's like something my Da would want to say only he wouldn't know how to say it.

THOMAS   Well, he would be entitled to say it. Your education requires a significant financial investment from him, I'm sure.

FRANCES   A significant financial investment. Nicely put. He'd say 'that young one is ating us out of house and home.'

THOMAS   Well, so you are.

FRANCES   Ah, but cute man, Paul. Do you know what he's been doing for the last eighteen years? Putting my Children's Allowance into an Insurance Policy. He has most of what I'll need stuck in it. How about that for the backward Paul?

THOMAS   Who said he was backward?

FRANCES   Ah, now, Thomas, like intellectually, he'd hardly blow

64

	you away. I'm only saying he's cute with money.
THOMAS	Well that's his contribution to the equation. Being intellectual isn't what he's about.
FRANCES	Ah, yeah but he can be a bit embarrassing.
THOMAS	How?
FRANCES	Well, he was at a Parent Teacher meeting one day. The maths teacher was saying that my numeracy was good and me Da said 'maybe she should do honours in numeracy so?' Honest to God, I was looking for a hole to get into.
THOMAS	He was merely fulfilling a parental function, to be an embarrassment to their children.
FRANCES	Well, he got there that day, alright.
THOMAS	Do you think have you ever been an embarrassment to them?
FRANCES	Me? No, of course not.
THOMAS	No? And if you were, do you think that they'd turn their backs on you?
FRANCES	Look, all I'm saying is he knows nothing really. Except about farming and money.
THOMAS	Not a bad combination. You're young, Frances and much as it pains me to say it and you to hear it; you have a lot to learn.
FRANCES	Yeah?
THOMAS	When I was fourteen my father was so ignorant I could hardly stand to have the old man around. But when I got to be twenty one I was astonished at how much he had learned in seven years.
FRANCES	Profound. Is it true?
THOMAS	I think so. I can't be sure. I'm quoting from Mark Twain.
FRANCES	Arrah, Thomas, you could have claimed that one as your own.
THOMAS	And then what would you think of me when you discovered that I had stolen it from Mark Twain? Tell me something?
FRANCES	What?
THOMAS	You always rattle on about your father. About his

	inadequacies. What about your mother?
FRANCES	My mother is a saint. She just does what she does, never indicating whether she wants to do it or not. Just keeps going. She seems what's the word, unflappable.
THOMAS	Have you noticed the swans down on the lake these times?
FRANCES	Yeah. There's a great mill of them there this year. Da says it's a sign of a bad winter ahead.
THOMAS	They remind me of your mother.
FRANCES	What?
THOMAS	Gliding beautifully along the top of the water whilst below the surface there are two feet paddling frantically to keep afloat. You must promise me, Frances, that you will mind your mother, be good to her. She has given you a lot of love. Now she may need some in return.
FRANCES	Ah, Ma is grand. She'll be alright. She knows how to handle herself. How to humour him.
THOMAS	She'll be alright but wouldn't it be nice if you could make it a little better than that?
FRANCES	You're a bit of an expert on handling parents.
THOMAS	Indeed I'm not. Both my parents died whilst I was quite young. That's why I always impress upon young people, indeed people of any age to cherish their parents. You won't always be eighteen, Frances, but as long as you have a parent alive there will always be someone who thinks that you are young.
FRANCES	God, Thomas, you're in awful philosophical mood today.
THOMAS	Yes and since I'm on a roll, I should talk to you about your father. No, perhaps not, can I tell you about my father?
FRANCES	You said he died when you were young?
THOMAS	Yes, but not before I knew he loved me.
FRANCES	Did he tell you?
THOMAS	No, not in so many words. He showed me.
FRANCES	How?
THOMAS	I was a very normal English child, interested in

football, cricket, that sort of thing. Toys weren't exactly hi-tech at that time and we were, by no means, wealthy. One Christmas, I must have been six or seven at the time, I got a lovely rubber ball in my stocking. It was the soft kind with which one could play indoors without creating havoc and I spent a lot of time playing against the wall in our living room. One day, after Christmas, my father was sitting by the fire, reading his Christmas Agatha Christie when the ball flew off my foot and went into the fire. My father, without hesitation, put his hand into the fire, took out the ball and went to the kitchen sink where he poured cold water on his hand and on the ball. He handed me the ball and said 'that was a close thing, Thomas; we nearly lost your ball.' I saw his hand, badly burned. The pain must have been excruciating but he never flinched.

FRANCES   Wow.

THOMAS   I have always used that story if ever asked to define unconditional love.

Pause

FRANCES   Thomas, you're a priest, aren't you?

THOMAS   What on earth put that notion in your head?

FRANCES   You speak in parables. Like a preacher.

THOMAS   Well, very few priests do that. Enough of this nonsense. This is your day. A day to celebrate your freedom.

FRANCES   Freedom? You make it sound, with all your preaching, like I'm just moving into the second part of my sentence.

THOMAS   I meant what I said to you about your mother.

FRANCES   Yeah, I know.

THOMAS   And your father?

FRANCES   What about him?

THOMAS   Frances, have you any idea how much he loves you?

FRANCES   Well, he never stuck his hand in the fire for me, that's for sure.

THOMAS   Are you sure? Has he never given you a present you didn't expect? A surprise or anything?

FRANCES	Are you joking? He never gave me a present in his life. I got a present at birthday and Christmas but that would be from the two of them and Mam would have bought it.
THOMAS	You are very hard on him.
FRANCES	Oh, come to think of it, he gave me the pencil case. I still have it, too
THOMAS	Pencil case?
FRANCES	This pencil case.

She takes fairly large, oak, carved pencil case from her bag and hands it to Thomas.

	Mind it, it's a ton weight.
THOMAS	It's beautiful. Where did he buy it?
FRANCES	He didn't buy it. He made it.
THOMAS	Made it?
FRANCES	Yes. He cut a branch off that old oak at the side of the house and he carved it from it.
THOMAS	The blasted oak.
FRANCES	Thomas, that's the first time I heard you swearing.
THOMAS	I wasn't swearing. That's what you call an oak tree that has been withered by storm or struck by lightening. A blasted oak. But this is beautiful. How long did it take him to do this?
FRANCES	Ah, he was foostering at it all summer. At night, like. He gave it to me the first day I went to Secondary School.
THOMAS	Look at the work. Look at those grooves. Look at the dowels. And with oak, Frances. Oak is the most difficult wood you could possibly attempt to do this with. Do you realise what this is?
FRANCES	A pencil case.
THOMAS	No, it's much more than that. This is a labour of love. A statement. This is your father saying, 'Frances, I love you' just as clearly as my father said it when he reached into the fire for my ball.
FRANCES	What?
THOMAS	Some men, Frances, can't say it. They can only show it. **Pause**

FRANCES	Thomas, you are making me feel about two inches tall.
THOMAS	I'm sorry. I didn't mean to.
FRANCES	No, it's ok.
	There is a moment while Frances lifts the pencil case and looks at it, as if for the first time.
	I've been a bit of a pig, haven't I?
THOMAS	Just a little bit, maybe.
FRANCES	God, I never thought of that case like that. I can see him now, he spent nights at that when he could have been having a pint in Annie's and a bit of craic with Pat Grant and my payback is to go around laughing at his lack of education.
THOMAS	*(quoting)*
	'Give me a spark of Nature's Fire,
	That's all the learning I desire.'
FRANCES	Who?
THOMAS	Robert Burns. He is saying that our nature is to love and to protect what we love.
FRANCES	You're not making me feel any better.
THOMAS	Did you ever buy him a present?
FRANCES	Arrah, you know, socks at Christmas, that sort of thing. Whatever Ma would pick out and buy. I'd sign the card.
THOMAS	You should buy him something yourself.
FRANCES	Yeah, I will. When I get paid the first week.
THOMAS	No. Do it today. Today is a special day for the two of you, happy for you and sad for him. It's a good day to show him that you are thinking of his feelings.
FRANCES	Jesus, do you know there's a lovely pipe set in Keaney's window, in Carrick. He'd love it. I wonder would Mr. Keaney give it to me until I get paid. It'd only be a week.
THOMAS	How much is it?
FRANCES	I don't know. It couldn't be anymore than twenty euro.
THOMAS	Well, then, let me lend you twenty euro.
FRANCES	No, I couldn't do that.
THOMAS	Why not? It's only a loan. You said yourself. Until next week.

FRANCES	Are you sure?
THOMAS	Of course.
	He gives her the money.
FRANCES	Thomas, you're a one off, a jewel. The nicest person I ever met.
THOMAS	Stop. Go now and get the present.
FRANCES	I'll go down by the rickety bridge, in case I meet him.
THOMAS	Yes, do. A good idea.
FRANCES	If he calls here, Thomas, you must swear not to tell him you saw me.
THOMAS	Alright.
FRANCES	Swear.
THOMAS	Alright. On my word of honour.
FRANCES	Good boy.
	She lifts the school bag but leaves the pencil case on the table.
THOMAS	Frances, I envy you today.
FRANCES	You envy me? Why?
THOMAS	Starting out in life. Full of optimism, dreams, hopes. Don't lose that outlook. Stay optimistic. No matter what happens believe in yourself always. Believe in life.
FRANCES	Thomas, I can never thank you for all you've done for me.
THOMAS	Nonsense, Frances, I've done nothing.
FRANCES	Yes you have. All the help you gave me with bits and pieces, the poetry and that. And what you said to me today.
THOMAS	It was nothing. I was going to say I'd do it for anyone but I don't know if that's true. You are a very special girl, Frances, don't ever forget that.
FRANCES	There now, didn't I tell you we'd become great mates. **Suddenly, they look at each other. There is a moment. They move towards each other, almost in a trance. Just when it seems they must touch, Frances gives a slight start of realisation and turns to leave. At exit she glances back at Thomas who remains transfixed. She leaves. A moment. Suddenly, Thomas goes into action. He removes the paper from the typewriter and leaves it on**

the table, covering the pencil case. He inserts a blank
sheet and begins to type as lights fade out.
A beat.
Lights come up. Thomas has finished typing and is
putting letter in envelope whilst cradling mobile phone
on his shoulder. He is in conversation.

THOMAS   Look, does there have to be a reason? I understood
the arrangement was that I could return whenever I
wished.
He listens.
Yes, well a number of things have happened. No,
nothing like that. It's just that this is not a place I
should remain in any longer.
A car is heard pulling up outside.
Car door bangs.
He listens.
Yes, I'll see the Auctioneer. I'm dropping the keys in on
my way past.
Well, I haven't made any significant improvements so I
expect it should fetch much the same as I paid for it.
Paul comes in. Thomas motions to him to sit down. He
sits. He is inebriated but not drunk.
Well, I'll call you again in the morning. No, I'll tell
you then. Look, somebody's just come in. I must go.
Alright. Yes. I'll talk to you then.
He finishes call.
Hello, Paul.

PAUL   Have you seen Frances?
THOMAS   Today?
PAUL   Yeah. Was she here?
THOMAS   Did she not have an exam?
PAUL   Only something short this morning. The last one.
THOMAS   Well, then, she probably went with her class to
celebrate. Unwind.
PAUL   She did. They were in the hotel but when I went
looking for her to bring her home; they told me she had
left to come here. To see you.
THOMAS   She might have thought I wasn't here and gone up

71

	home.
PAUL	She's not at home.
THOMAS	She must be still in town.
PAUL	Maybe.
	(making to leave)
	I'll go back down and see if I can find her.
THOMAS	I'm sure she's quite safe.
PAUL	*(coming back)*
	Why shouldn't she be?
THOMAS	Of course. No reason. Can I get you something? Cup of tea? Coffee perhaps?
PAUL	No, I want no tea or coffee.
THOMAS	I'm sorry, Paul, I have nothing stronger.
PAUL	I want nothing from you, Englishman, only that you leave my daughter alone.
THOMAS	Sorry?
PAUL	You leave Frances alone.
THOMAS	Paul, I haven't touched your daughter.
PAUL	No and you won't either. I'm her father, you remember that. What do you think it's like for me to go into a crowd of youngsters below in the hotel and when I ask them where Frances is they tell me she's gone up to see her boyfriend and they're giggling. Laughing at me. I won't have it. I'm her father and I won't have it.
THOMAS	I assure you, Paul, my only interest in Frances is to see her do well. To get the best possible results she can.
PAUL	For what?
THOMAS	For what? How do you mean?
PAUL	Best results for what? So that she can leave. Go away. Leave this place.
THOMAS	Paul, it is the nature of things that young people leave. There is nothing here for Frances. She must go.
PAUL	I didn't.
THOMAS	You are the exception that proves the rule.
PAUL	What the fuck does that mean?
THOMAS	Your trade, your profession meant that you stayed. Without that you'd have gone. Look at Pat's family, Brussels, Birmingham.

Pause

PAUL   What's to become of us at all?

THOMAS   What's wrong Paul?

PAUL   What are we going to do without her? What am I going to do without her?

THOMAS   She'll be home regularly, Paul.

PAUL   No, she won't. Oh, she'll intend to be, alright, but once she shakes the dust of this place off her feet, fuck the back near it she'll come. Only when she has to, Christmas time and to bury us.

THOMAS   Paul, you love her too much.

PAUL   Love her too much? How could I love her too much? What else have I to love?

THOMAS   Mary.

PAUL   That's different.

THOMAS   How? How is it different?

PAUL   I don't know. It's just different.

THOMAS   You must let her go.

PAUL   Don't you think I know that? It's how to let her go that I don't know.

Pause

I always wanted a son. I think that's only natural. My father before me would have wanted a son. You feel you're fighting for something, in a place like this, if you have a son to take over, to carry on the fight. So I wanted a son. Right up to the minute her mother handed her to me and I held her in my arms. From that time on, I never wanted anything else only her. I loved her from the first second I held her. I've spent the last eighteen years codding myself that this day wouldn't come. That she might settle for what was here. Have you any idea what it's like to be working for something and know that you're going to lose it anyway in the end? Codding myself. I knew all along that Frances wouldn't settle for less. We both knew, me and Mary. But sure what else did we know. That's feckin' education for you now. Once they think there's something better, that's it. They're gone.

THOMAS	It's life, Paul. You must accept life. Everyone gets crosses. It's how you shoulder the cross that marks you out as a man.
PAUL	What is going to happen to us? What? I know it's daft, it's selfish. I should be proud about her but all I can think of is what's going to happen to me? Will I finish up like Pat Grant doing crosswords all day with the widow and jigsaws all night at home in the house, not able to sleep.
THOMAS	Paul, you're a long way from that. For one thing you have Mary. She's not going.
PAUL	Will she stay?
THOMAS	Why shouldn't she stay?
PAUL	Pat's wife didn't. I'm afraid. I'm afraid, Thomas. Mary might see no reason to stay.
THOMAS	You think that because you have been obsessed with Frances. When she leaves, you and Mary will be thrown back together and rediscover yourselves.
PAUL	You think it's as easy as all that, don't you? Just like reading it out of a book. Like saying the war is over and forget about the battles you won and lost.
THOMAS	Your life is about the future. It has to be.
PAUL	Maybe. Anyway, I'd better go back down and see if I can find her
THOMAS	Try home first. She may be back by now.
PAUL	Back?
THOMAS	You know, from town. If you missed her before.
PAUL	Right. I'll go so. Look, Thomas, I'm sorry for...you know.
THOMAS	It's alright. I understand. *(as **Paul** exits)* Paul.
PAUL	What?
THOMAS	There's something I want to tell you but I must ask you not to say anything about it until tomorrow.
PAUL	What?
THOMAS	I'm leaving. Tonight. This evening.
PAUL	Leaving? Why? What happened?

THOMAS	Just something that came up that requires my attention.
PAUL	Bit sudden, isn't it?
THOMAS	Yes, well that's the way, I'm afraid.
PAUL	But you'll be back?
THOMAS	No, I won't.
PAUL	But the place? Here? What about that?
THOMAS	I'm giving it to the auctioneer.
PAUL	God, that was quick.
THOMAS	Somebody asked me to promise them something. I thought I could. Now I suddenly find that I can't keep my promise if I stay here any longer. So I must go.
PAUL	You're talking in riddles.
THOMAS	Am I? Sorry, but that's as much as I can say. But Paul, I want you to give this note to Frances. Tomorrow. It's nothing, just a valediction, a farewell. Since I won't see her.
PAUL	*(taking and pocketing the letter)* Alright. So you're leaving, too. Hah? The deserted village. Is that a poem?
THOMAS	Yes. Goldsmith.
PAUL	So what about this? The writing? **He lifts the paper from on top of the pencil case. He sees the pencil case. He looks at Thomas and the back at the case. A moment.** Jesus, what have you done? That's her pencil case. What have you done to her, you bastard?
THOMAS	Look, Paul, I'm not supposed to tell you but there's a very simple explanation.
PAUL	What have you done to my child?
THOMAS	Paul, will you listen to me. She's alright. She left here to go to town.
PAUL	Jesus, you liar you. When I asked you if you had seen her you said you hadn't. And when I came here, you're getting ready to leave. And a letter...
THOMAS	I tell you, Paul, on the word of God, she's gone to buy a present for you. A new pipe.
PAUL	A present for me? Are you sick? She never bought me

anything in her life. Where would she get the money?

THOMAS I lent her twenty euro.

PAUL *(grabbing Paul)*
And what had she to do for that, you fucking pervert.
Suddenly Paul pulls Thomas down onto the table, lifts
the pencil case and in the same movement and strikes
Thomas a full blow on the side of his head. Thomas
falls. Paul stands, stunned by his action. He sees the
pencil case in his hand and lets it fall to the ground as
lights go to black out.

The change of set back to the dilapidated bar should
be covered either by music or rainfall which continues
through the epilogue.

SCENE ELEVEN

(Epilogue)

Jackson's Bar.
Dawson and Pat Kelly enter.
It is raining.

DAWSON	So, what happened?
PAT	Arrah, what do you think happened? There was a court case. Hi, what are we doing back here?
DAWSON	Out of the rain. And it just seems natural. Finish the story where you started. Anyway, there was a court case.
PAT	Paul was charged with manslaughter. 'Twas thought for a while he'd be charged with murder but, no. He got three years in jail. He was out in less than eighteen months.
DAWSON	He got off light.
PAT	How?
DAWSON	Eighteen months.
PAT	Three years he got. I suppose he got off lighter than Hopkinson anyway. He'd probably have got more only it was an Englishman.
DAWSON	Why do you say that?
PAT	Well, there was no one to speak up for the dead man. To make a hullabaloo. Demand more.
DAWSON	Still, I suppose no matter what jail he got he's serving a life sentence. In his head, anyway.
PAT	Maybe.
DAWSON	And the wife and child?
PAT	She saw her chance. The wife. He wasn't inside five minutes when she had the place for sale. Need to be near to him, she said. Ye're crowd bought it and she went off in a cloud of dust and never set foot here since, only the once, for the widow's funeral.

DAWSON	The widow?
PAT	The woman that owned this place. Annie Jackson. She got a pain. Went to Dublin. Riddled. Lasted six weeks. The craytur. Grand decent woman she was. God knows, she hadn't it aisy either.
DAWSON	What about the daughter. Did she do law?
PAT	Arrah, how could she do law after what he did? She got married about Dublin and had a clatter of children and the mother looks after them while she's working in some office. Poor Paul worked in a factory up to the pension. Imagine a man like that stuck in a factory. Smothering. Lord, what a waste.
DAWSON	Why was the place burned?
PAT	Settle for the news you got, now, boy.
	Pause
DAWSON	The whole thing was a waste wasn't it?
PAT	That's life. That happens if you don't let go of something that's pulling away from you. It'll bring all with it.
DAWSON	Any sign of you letting go?
PAT	Hah?
DAWSON	I suppose there's little point in asking you the usual question? You won't sell?
PAT	How do you know?
DAWSON	Arrah, you're as happy as Larry.
PAT	Being happy as Larry is fine as long as Larry is happy. No, I won't sell
DAWSON	I'll be back again, you know. Or someone else.
PAT	Oh, I know you will. I'll still be here.
DAWSON	What's the point?
PAT	The point is it's what I know. It's my place. I'm entitled to live here, to die here, if I want to. I know I can go to England or America to live anytime I want to but this is where I want to be.
DAWSON	America?
PAT	Aye. One of the lads is over there this years. Has his own construction company.
DAWSON	He's doing well.

PAT	Oh, I think so. The only thing I notice is that he knew everything when he was here but he seems to be only guessing since he went to the States. It's I guess this and I guess that. But, anyway, I have them places if I ever need them. It's a poor mouse that has only one hole.
DAWSON	Do they not want you to go? Your wife and daughter? Surely they want you over?
PAT	Maybe they do. Maybe they don't. It works grand the way it is. I go across, they come over and we never stay around long enough to get fed up with each other. Sure we're talking on the internet ten times a day anyway.
DAWSON	What do you think you're achieving? Staying here on your own?
PAT	I'm living the way I want to. Not the way people think I should.
DAWSON	After your time...
PAT	*(interrupting)*
	After my time they can do what they like with it. At least they'll have a choice. I'll leave them that, if nothing else.
DAWSON	You're a bloody awkward man.
PAT	Because I won't co-operate, is it? Hah? There was no instructions on the box I came in and there'll be no address on the one I leave in so I have to make it up as I go along. I'm afraid, Mr. Dawson, like the fellas before you, you'll have to go back to your lord and master and tell him you failed.
DAWSON	I'm only doing my job.
PAT	I'm only doing my job, the soldier said as he hammered the nails into the cross. You know, after World War Two, years after, they found this Japanese soldier in the jungle, still fighting the war. And they said to him, 'come out to fuck outa that, you daft little bollix, the war is long over.' So he came out. But they were telling him lies. The war wasn't over. It was just that the enemy had changed. So I'm still here in the jungle but I know that the war will never be over and I'll keep going as long as I'm able.

DAWSON	And then?
PAT	And then? And then I'll still keep going. Now leave it at that. Come down to the house and I'll give you a glass of the finest poitin you ever drank.
DAWSON	Poitin?
PAT	Aye. And then when you go back to the smoke you can tell them you drank jungle juice with the Japanese soldier and there's no sign of the hoor surrendering. Come on.

He exits.
Dawson goes to follow but stops at exit and looks back at bar. He returns and, with care and reverence he replaces the furniture as he found it at the start of the play. He takes a last look and exits.

FADE ON EXIT

END

Unforgiven

CHARACTERS

PJ   Bachelor farmer. Late forties.

SEAMIE   PJ's brother. Late thirties.

MARY   Neighbour of PJ and Eamonn. Early forties.

EAMONN   Brother of PJ and Eamonn. Living in
                California.Mid forties.

OUTLINE OF SCENES

The action of the play takes place in the kitchen of PJ and Seamie's house over a period of a one month. Time—the present.

ACT ONE

SCENE ONE   A June mid-morning..

SCENE TWO   Late Afternoon, the same day.

SCENE THREE   Afternoon, two day's later.

ACT TWO

SCENE ONE   Mid-morning, one week later..

SCENE TWO   Mid-day, three weeks later..

SCENE THREE   Later that night.

ACT ONE

SCENE ONE

It is a June afternoon. A farmhouse kitchen/living room. The room is an untidy bachelor abode. Upstage centre is a scullery with back door. Upstage left is a door leading to bedroom. Left centre is a fireplace containing a black Stanley range. There is a large pot of stew on the range. Between the door and fireplace is an armchair. Downstage right is a door leading to second bedroom. Centre stage is a table with three chairs. In the corner, upstage right, is a modern wide-screen television and video player. It is the only modern item in the room and it is surrounded from floor to ceiling with videotapes of all descriptions, filed in a haphazard manner. At least 400 videos.

PJ   *(emerging from bedroom)*
Alright, I will. I will
Sound from bedroom.
(going back)
What?
How do I know whether he will or not? I can't make him. Right. I'll ask him. Again.
(coming out)
God give me patience.
(speaking back to room)
If you don't die soon, I'll feckin strangle you. Wouldn't you think you'd just throw in the towel and be done with it and not have me scalded looking after you these twelve months? You're not going to get better so you might as well feck off and stop persecuting us. But no, you won't, will you? You won't, 'cause you're as thick as the top of a hatchet. Waiting. Hanging on. Waiting

to see will Seamie talk to you. Well he won't. He has
no notion of talking to you, only the wan word, 'cause,
Daddy dear, thick and all as you are, you have one son
thicker. That Seamie buck won't cave in and speak to
you. So you might as well go. Up or down or whichever
will have you. And not have me here like an eejit trying
to keep the peace between ye. It's like I have no life at
all. And that other hoor of a son of yours, beyond in
California, won't come near you either.
(in American accent)
"Bell me, PJ, when he expires, I've no need to see him
prior to that."
Well, don't worry, PJ'll bell the whole country when he
expires. If I'm not dead myself before the hoor.
Goes to back door and shouts out.
Wan Word. Wan Word. Seamie. Come in, will you. He
wants you.
(returning)
Some family. I'm like Our Lord on the Cross. Crucified
between two thieves. Ah, but PJ will get his revenge in
the end. For you'll die and as soon as you do, Mary and
myself will marry and the Seamie buck can feck off outa
here. Maybe the Yank will bring him over to California.
He could put him on the Oprah Winfrey Show over
there. The man that never says more than wan word.
Noise from bedroom—a call.
Die, I said
(voice from bedroom—What?)
Aye, I said. He's coming.
Goes to back door and shouts out.
Will you come in, you balawan, before he gets up and
goes out for you.
(returning)
By God, there'll be some clearance round here when
you do the decent thing and die. It'll be worse than if
Clint Eastwood and The Terminator rode into town the
same day. I'll be shot of the lot of you and Mary and
myself can live happy ever after and not be listening to

you moaning like a donny bullock above in the room and the other tulip going round with more chips on his shoulder than Burger King would sell in a week.

Seamie enters.

SEAMIE   What?

PJ   What? He's looking for you. That's what.

SEAMIE   So?

PJ   Well, will you go up to him and not have my arse annoyed listening to him.

SEAMIE   Right.

PJ   Wan Word.

SEAMIE   What?

PJ   Will you talk to him?

SEAMIE   No.

PJ   What kind of a thick fucker are you? Isn't this going on long enough? The man is dying. I don't care what went on between ye. He's your father. Can you not give him a dying wish? Talk to him. Will you?

SEAMIE   No.

PJ   Christ, will you not talk to him for my sake. Your brother. I'm at my wit's end. He thinks I can make you talk to him, say more than the wan word. Will you?

SEAMIE   Never.

PJ   Well, that the pair of ye may die roaring.

SEAMIE   Right.

PJ   Go up, anyway. Give me a rest from him.

SEAMIE   Sound

Goes into bedroom.

PJ   *(getting plate from pantry and pouring stew from pot which he eats during the following)*

Oh, Mammy, why didn't you bring Seamie with you the night you died and not have his father blaming him for killing you? I suppose if you'd done that he'd have blamed me for killing the two of you. It wouldn't have been his fault anyway. Well, I'll live to see the pair of them off the premises.

Mary enters.

MARY   God save all in this house.

89

PJ	God, Mary, don't say that in case he does. I'm all that's worth saving here. How are you today?
MARY	I'm twice as good as when I was half as bad. How are things in ER?
PJ	The same as they were yesterday. And, I suppose the same as they'll be tomorrow. The pair of them is above. My father, like a burst melodeon, wind coming out of every hole, pleading with Seamie to talk to him and Seamie saying nothing, beyond the wan word.
MARY	It's as daft as two bald men fighting over a comb. Wouldn't you think that Seamie would talk to him and him dying?
PJ	I suppose he doesn't forget the beating he took.
MARY	Still, twenty five years is a long time just to be saying the wan word.
PJ	It takes a fairly thick man to do it.
MARY	It should never have happened.
PJ	What? The beating?
MARY	The beating.
PJ	Ah, now, Mary, you can aisy say it should never have happened. If Seamie hadn't talked back to him, the old fella wouldn't have beaten him.
MARY	Arrah, what age was Seamie? Fourteen? Fifteen? How could he know the difference at that age?
PJ	Well, he should have.
MARY	How? Did his father ever beat him before?
PJ	No.
MARY	Well, then, he could hardly have expected it to happen, could he?
PJ	I suppose our father lost control.
MARY	How do you mean?
PJ	What with everything, I suppose something snapped. He must have been out of control because the strength of him was wicked. I tried to pull him away but he flung me across the kitchen. It was the first time I was ever afraid of my father but he had the look of a drowning man in his eyes. Jesus, it was frightening.
MARY	There was nothing you could do, PJ.

PJ	I tried, Mary, honest to God, I tried but the man was out of his mind. And you'd think it was a natural enough thing for a father to say to a son that was after answering him back. To say if he heard more than wan word out of him again he'd strangle him. You think it was natural enough and wouldn't pass much heed of it.
MARY	He didn't know that his son was as thick as himself and wouldn't say more than wan word since.
PJ	How could anyone expect that of a gossoon that age?
MARY	Or that he'd be able to do it. To keep it up.
PJ	Aye, well he met his match in Seamie.
MARY	He sure did. I wonder does anyone younger than him know his name at all. Nearly all just call him Wan Word.
PJ	That's some claim to fame. Christ, this house is a laughing stock for the outside world with the pair of them.
MARY	Still, it was an awful act. To beat a cub like that.
PJ	It was, I suppose. But, sometimes, when you're that age you're looking for a beating. And I think Daddy must have been at his wit's end with the three of us.
MARY	How?
PJ	I think because Mammy died having Seamie, he always blamed Seamie for killing her. I think he felt he'd have been better to lose the child and save the wife.
MARY	You sound like you're excusing it.
PJ	No, Mary, indeed I'm not. It's me that's paying for it. It was an awful beating. An awful act. I'm only trying to explain it. If he got any value out of it, he paid dearly for it. Between Wan Word not talking and Eamonn shagging off to America.
MARY	Any word from Eamonn?
PJ	I rang him last night. He won't come until he has to.
MARY	Another thick man. Mammy says you're the only one with a bit of the mother in you. That other pair, she says, you'd think the auld stallion had them all on his own.
PJ	How is the Mammy the day?

91

MARY	Same as ever. No more than what's above in the room, she'll die when she's ready.
PJ	There's not a lot left of her now.
MARY	No, but she wants to live on.
PJ	Why?
MARY	Ah, why do any of us want to live? Afraid of dying, maybe. And you'd never know what would be going on in her head as well. She mightn't want to be the last to go.
PJ	Well, now, she has no need to be afraid of dying.
MARY	Maybe.
	Pause
	PJ, do you think there's anything after death?
PJ	Well, I hope that there's more than there is before it.
	Pause
	I don't know what's tomorrow going to be like? Did you get the forecast?
MARY	Aye. Light winds and occasional showers.
PJ	Who gave it out?
MARY	Gerald Fleming.
PJ	Well, that's alright then. Fleming does have great weather. You'd know well he studied it. Them young wans are dangerous giving out the weather. Grinning out at you and trying to take your mind off it. You know well when they start smiling that it's going to be pissing down on you and that they don't give a shite 'cause they're not going to get wet anyway.
MARY	I wish it would clear up until Scraper would come and finish the new room. Bad weather is a great excuse for him.
PJ	God, that room is going on a long time, Mary.
MARY	When we gave Scraper the job I thought he said six to eight weeks. He must have said sixty eight weeks.
PJ	If Scraper was making crosses, Our Lord would still be alive.
MARY	*(rising)*
	I'd better go up and see himself, anyway.
PJ	Tear ahead, she said, they're Mammies.

MARY	Does he want anything up. Water or anything?
PJ	Don't worry. He'll tell you quick enough if he does. You'll be lucky to get a word in edgeways with that pair.
	Seamie enters from bedroom.
MARY	Well, Wan Word.
SEAMIE	Mary.
MARY	How is he now?
SEAMIE	Poorly.
MARY	Well, compared with yesterday, like.
SEAMIE	Worse.
MARY	Weaker?
SEAMIE	Thicker.
PJ	Well you'd be the boy with the qualifications for measuring thickness.
SEAMIE	Maybe.
MARY	Well, I'll see if I can knock any auld craic out of him.
	She goes to bedroom.
	Seamie moves to go outside.
PJ	Hi, boy, wait up a second.
SEAMIE	Why?
PJ	I want to talk to you. Sit down there now and listen to this.
SEAMIE	Hurry.
PJ	Why? Is there one of The Corrs waiting for you without on the tractor. You'll sit there 'till I'm finished.
SEAMIE	*(sitting)*
	Right.
PJ	Now, look here, you're nearly forty years of age and it's time you started acting your age. That's your father that's dying up there and love him or hate him; he's still your father. You'll only ever have one of them, boy, so you'd better make the most of it. Now, I know you think you're entitled to do what you're doing. Maybe you are. And it takes a fair tough man to do it. But it takes an even tougher man to stop doing it. And to know when to stop. That man up there is staving off death these months to be right with you before he goes.

93

	It's not right. It's not fair on him. Nor on me. You've made your point. Now it's time to let the old man go. **Pause** *(being reasonable)* Look at it this way. If you don't talk to him you might regret it for the rest of your life. If you do talk, you'll never be sorry for you'll know you did the right thing. Do you know what I mean?
SEAMIE	Aye.
PJ	Good man. So you'll talk to him.
SEAMIE	No.
PJ	*(raging)* Well, that your two balls may get caught in the front wheel of your bike. You're the thickest bastard ever walked the face of the Earth.
SEAMIE	Second
PJ	What?
SEAMIE	*(pointing to bedroom)* First. **Mary comes in from bedroom.**
MARY	Wan Word, he wants you again.
SEAMIE	Why?
MARY	Ah, why do you think? To discuss the Common Agricultural Policy? Go on up to him. You mightn't have to go up much more.
SEAMIE	Sound.
MARY	Wan Word.
SEAMIE	Aye.
MARY	Will you do something for me?
SEAMIE	Surely.
MARY	Will you talk to him? **Seamie nods and goes into bedroom.**
PJ	Devil the talk that fella will do.
MARY	He might.
PJ	I'm after trying him, soft and hard. He won't budge.
MARY	The old man told me something. I told him to say it to Seamie. It might work.
PJ	What?

94

MARY	Ah, nothing. Anyway, it'll have to happen soon. He's fading fast.
PJ	He is, isn't he? He's a wicked colour. Hah?
MARY	Well, if you were getting a room ready for the station, you wouldn't bring him into the paint shop and say 'gimme a tin the colour of that' and that's for sure. Will I make tea?
PJ	Do you want some yourself?
MARY	Do you think I'd be making it for you?
PJ	Go on, so. It'll be practice for you.
MARY	*(laughing)* 'Twill. I'm practised enough, thanks.
PJ	So you reckon we're nearly there. With your man, like.
MARY	He'll die anytime, PJ. The fight is gone out of him and he knows himself he's a losing ticket.
PJ	Well, he's my father and I shouldn't say it but it will be great release for us all.
MARY	You'll miss him now, all the same.
PJ	Like a sore tooth.
MARY	Did you ever notice, when you go to the dentist to get a tooth pulled, everyone asks you after 'how's the tooth'? It's the same at a funeral, praying for the dead when it's the living we should be worried about. Feck what's gone, look after what's left behind.
PJ	Ah, Mary, that's just it. You can fairly put what a man would be thinking into words. **Pause** Boys, it will be great when he's gone, all the same.
MARY	*(quickly)* Any good videos lately?
PJ	Did you ever see American Beauty?
MARY	No.
PJ	Jaysus, that's a wild country, America. It's fierce what they get up to. Auld fells chasing after young wans and everything.
MARY	Yeah? Sure they do be at that here too.
PJ	Aye, but in America they do catch up with them. At least in the videos.

MARY	You should go over. You might catch one. Maybe a black cailin. That would put the chat off Wan Word altogether.
PJ	I'd sooner cut silage with a scissors than go to America. They'd knife you for nothing out there. Would you like to go?
MARY	Only for a holiday. I wouldn't mind a holiday. But I couldn't stay.
PJ	No more than myself, you got badly spanceled here. With your mother.
MARY	Arrah, I did and I didn't. I wasn't going leaving anyway and she didn't get sick on purpose. What I'll do after she dies is a different matter. Be they bad or mad a brother or a sister is a useful article. I have neither.
PJ	Nor a husband.
MARY	*(again quickly)* So you watched American…what is it?
PJ	American Beauty. Kevin Spacey. And a good auld cowboy too, after. I forget the name of it. It's there in the machine. There was men shot out of a face in it. I'll come down after a while to see if there's anything needs doing around your place, Mary.
MARY	No need. Wan Word was down already.
PJ	The hoor. That's where he went on the tractor. I thought he was gone to the Co-op. What did he do?
MARY	Feck all. Mammy was asleep this morning so I got out to the cattle myself. The fresh air was welcome.
PJ	You're a mighty woman that can do it all. You won't know yourself if you get a man full time. Like a partner. Husband, like.
MARY	What would that be only another beast to be fed morning and night? I'm alright as long as I have good neighbours.
PJ	They're disappearing on you too. There's no sign of anyone buying Corky's place?
MARY	There was someone looking at it last week but I'd say it's only fit for forestry.
PJ	'Twas a good place 'till Corky got it. Christ, talk about

laziness.

MARY	A philosopher never made a farmer.
PJ	Ah, now, he could have stirred himself a bit more.
MARY	And he had everyone else around him as bad as himself. He had a cat down there and she was that lazy that our cat used to have to go down to catch the mice for her.
PJ	And still with all the minding on himself, he went quick in the end.
MARY	Well, it was the first thing he ever did quick in his life.
PJ	The forestry, you think?
MARY	Afraid so.
PJ	We'll soon be all that's left.
MARY	Arrah, if all comes to all, I can put an ad in Ireland's Own.
PJ	Christ, do not, Mary, you'd never know what kind of a gobshite would pull up on your street.
MARY	I'm only codding.
	(laughing to herself)
	Did you hear the one Maurice Kelly told the women at the Bingo last week?
PJ	No, and I'm not sure I want to. Maurice's do be fairly hairy.
MARY	This wan put an ad in 'sexy lady requires similar male to satisfy her requirements.'
PJ	In Ireland's Own?
MARY	Ah, not at all. Will you shut up and listen. Anyway, her door bell rings and she goes out and there's this wee fella bobbing around on the step. No arms, no legs and he says 'I saw your ad.' Your wan bursts out laughing and says 'what makes you think you could satisfy my requirements?' and he says 'how do you think I rang the bell?'
	Mary explodes laughing. PJ looks bemused.
PJ	How could he ring the door bell if he had no arms or legs?
MARY	Oh, God, PJ, you're as innocent as the Birmingham Six. Keep on that beard for if a Bishop met you without

	it he'd think you were for Confirmation.
PJ	I'll be a more likely candidate for Extreme Unction by the time this buck in the bed takes his leave.
MARY	You'll need to make arrangements. Contact Eamonn and all that.
PJ	That'll be alright. Although it'll go hard on the hoor to come back near the place.
MARY	Long time gone.
PJ	Another casualty of the row between Wan Word and the boss.
MARY	Bailed out.
PJ	And never came back.
MARY	Strange.
PJ	Not a word you'd use to describe anything that'd happen in this house.
MARY	No, but I mean that he wouldn't come back and his sons that had no attachment to the place, would.
PJ	Man, that was a good one. Pair of bucks landing in the door to see their grandfather.
MARY	Swore us to secrecy.
PJ	Said Eamonn never wanted them to see where he came from. Some Irishman, that, what? Two grand young bucks, too.
MARY	Fine Lads. Shane and Patrick. Eamonn's wife must be a fairly strong woman.
PJ	Why?
MARY	You may be sure it wasn't Eamonn that put the two Irish names on them. He doesn't seem to have much time for the auld sod. I don't know did I like the way they went against their father's wishes.
PJ	What?
MARY	Coming here when their father didn't want them to.
PJ	Well that kind of behaviour sort of runs in this family.
MARY	Still, 'twill be nice to see Eamonn after all these years. Even though I never forgot him.
PJ	Don't tell me you had a notion of him?
MARY	What if I had?
PJ	Arrah, Mary, sure you were only a child when he left.

MARY	I'll take that as a compliment. Liar. I was near the same age as him.
PJ	Plenty more of them compliments where that came from. God, Mary, it's great to have a friendly face around the place. I can tell you that pair would take it out of you. There's days here and if I was a lamppost, a dog wouldn't piss on me.
MARY	I know, PJ, but there's good times coming.
PJ	Amen to that.
	Seamie enters from bedroom.
MARY	Well.
SEAMIE	Dead.
	Pause
	Seamie laughs.
PJ	What are you laughing at?
SEAMIE	*(roars)*
	Victory

FADE TO END OF SCENE

SCENE TWO

Later the same day. PJ is standing at the range. Mary sits at the table, copying from Irish Independent.

MARY   *(as she writes)*
After a long illness, borne with great courage and dignity.

PJ   By PJ.

MARY   What?

PJ   Borne with great courage and dignity by PJ.

MARY   Ah, feck off.

PJ   Well, who had to bear it? With them two bucks. At least Jesus had one good thief with him on the cross.

MARY   Look it, will you shut up and let me finish this.

PJ   What's keeping them bucks up there? You wouldn't think it would take that long to lay out a corpse.

MARY   Do you want him looking like Homer Simpson or do you want him laid out properly? And are you sure you want to bring him to the funeral home? Hah? You don't want him waked here?

PJ   No, bejaysus. Every auld hoor in the country up sniffing round the place, looking for news and maybe Wan Word getting up to his tricks like he did the time of the station.

MARY   What was that?

PJ   Ah, nothing.

MARY   PJ?

PJ   Arrah, it was Mrs. Lyons. You know the way that auld bitch'd be, giving orders and wanting things. He was making a mug of tea for her and she told him to put three spoons of sugar in it. Not, indeed, that that would sweeten her anything. So I find your man in the back kitchen with a packet of Glauber salts that was in the house since one time the auld man was constipated and him lorrying it into the mug along with the sugar.

MARY	And did you not stop him?
PJ	Why?
MARY	God, you're as bad as he is. And did she drink it?
PJ	She washed down a round of egg and onion sandwiches with it. She wasn't seen for three days after. Stuck to the bucket. So I think the old man might be safer below in the funeral home for Wan Word might take a notion and paint a moustache on him with a marker.
MARY	And what did Mrs. Lyons say when she found out?
PJ	She didn't. Find out, like. Well, we were hardly going to tell her. She put it down to bad eggs in the sandwiches.
MARY	And did you never tell anyone?
PJ	No. And you never heard it either. Well, I did tell The Master one night the two of us were drunk.
MARY	And?
PJ	And what?
MARY	What did he say?
PJ	He said at least Young Lyons wouldn't be stuck for slurry for a while.
	Seamie enters from bedroom.
SEAMIE	Whiskey.
PJ	In the top press out there. Are they near finished?
SEAMIE	Aye.
MARY	They must be getting to the tasty bit when they're looking for drink.
SEAMIE	Shaving.
PJ	It'll be the first time ever he didn't cut himself.
	Seamie goes back into bedroom.
MARY	Now how's this? Peacefully at his residence.
PJ	Aye
MARY	Deeply regretted by his loving sons PJ, Eamonn and Seamus and a wide circle of friends.
PJ	Hah!
MARY	Shut up. Reposing at Kelly's funeral home from 5pm to 7pm on Wednesday with removal for 7.30pm to St. Kevin's Church, Ballyoran. Funeral mass at 11 am on Thursday with burial immediately afterwards in adjoining cemetery.

PJ	English and American papers please copy.
MARY	What?
PJ	English and American papers please copy. You always see that when there's some of the family abroad.
MARY	Oh, Jesus. I forgot about that. That's fierce important. I can just see Arnold Swarzenneger in the Governor's office in California reading that and saying to the wife 'I think that's Eamonn's father that's dead. That's a funeral on us.' And she's one of the Kennedy's so she'll say 'I must ring Teddy; he'll want to go to that.' English and American papers please copy my arse.
PJ	Well, I do see it.
MARY	Well you won't see it on this. There's enough laughing at ye without giving them another excuse. Hadn't your father the cure for the burn?
PJ	He had.
MARY	And did he leave it to anyone?
PJ	He brought it with him for he'll need it where he's gone.
MARY	Wait 'till you see, you'll miss him all the same.
PJ	I suppose I will. A father is a father when all is said and done but he was hard to explain to anyone that didn't know him and the way he was with Wan Word wasn't right. No father should be like that with a son. And he had the place in such an upheaval that no one could do anything, bring anyone around the place. It was hard to convince anyone that you were sane yourself and you living with two lunatics.
MARY	PJ, don't be so hard on your father. For these few days, anyhow. Let him off in peace. Let the people think there's someone sorry after him.
	Pause
PJ	I'm sorry after him.
MARY	Well, then...
PJ	You get into a kind of way of being one way about a thing and that's it. I know he regretted every single day what happened with Seamie and I know he tried every way known to man to get him back. I know that but I

	couldn't be taking sides.
MARY	The two of them suffered out of it.
PJ	Remember there, a few years ago, when the club won the County Championship. First time ever. There was fierce excitement. You know the way it is, when something like that happens, everyone is in great humour and any auld differences are forgotten for a while. There's men with their arms around each other that'd have been sculling other a few days before. We were all in The Pipers, grand feed of drink. The old man, Seamie, all hands in great form. We got back to the house and I made a sup of tea and our father tried every angle to break through to Seamie. But no. Nothing. How he held out, I don't know, but he did. They went to bed and I got stuck in an auld jigsaw for if I went straight away I'd only have to be getting up in an hour anyway. And then I heard the sobbing from the room.
MARY	Sobbing?
PJ	My father. First it was just sobbing and then full blast crying. I thought he'd never stop.
MARY	Did you not go up to him?
PJ	How could I? The man would be out of his mind if he thought anyone heard him. Anyway, I was in such a state myself that I felt like bringing in the shotgun and doing away with the two of them. Only I thought of Mammy and what she'd say.
MARY	Ah, poor PJ.
PJ	And I got to wondering how many nights he was like that and no one to hear him. So, I'm sorry after him. For I know what way he's gone and what he has to face. But that's that. That's finished now. And there will be changes around here. And they'll be changes for the better, Mary.
MARY	Right. Good. Well, we'll see.
	Seamie enters from bedroom.
SEAMIE	Done.
MARY	Does he look well?

SEAMIE	Powerful.
PJ	Aye.
SEAMIE	Closing.
	He goes back to bedroom.
MARY	Go up, PJ. You'd better pass him fit for inspection.
PJ	Arrah, he'll be alright.
MARY	Go up. Keep an eye on that buck. Remember Mrs. Lyons.
PJ	Alright, I will. They'll want a hand bringing him out anyway. Will you do the chairs?
MARY	I will.
	PJ exits to bedroom.
MARY	*(while upending each chair in the kitchen)*
	May your spirit leave this house now, old man, for there is no seat for you in this kitchen any more. May The Lord have mercy on your soul.
	She blesses herself as lights fade down to end of scene.

SCENE THREE

The day of the funeral. Eamonn is speaking on mobile phone and pacing the room. He is a well dressed and well groomed American.

EAMONN   Well, it's like I told you, honey, funerals over here are much less private than in California. You get a hell of a lot of people offering sympathy to the bereaved. I shook hands with a lot of folk today that I'm sure I should have known but I hadn't a clue who they were. And then you get a lot of spectators. You know, people who come just to be seen. Yeah, I suppose my presence created some interest. The way they say it in Ireland is 'I wouldn't know I ever saw you before' which is rich when I don't remember them anyway. Other people don't think they age at all themselves. Well, honey, it's done and dusted now and we're left to ourselves at the end of it all.

My brothers? Some boys, those two. Gee, all that's missing around this house is guys in white coats to give them medication three times daily. Of course, they think they're perfectly sane.

He listens.

Yeah?

Well, you tell me. One guy who has never said more than one word for the past twenty five years and another who has what I can only describe as a shrine to video recording in the corner of the living room. Jeez, honey, these guys are as mad as a bag of frogs. They had a dog here and you know how faithful a dog is. Well, this one left. Bailed out. Disappeared. Probably was afraid he was going to become as daft as this pair. Boys ok? Good. Fine. Well, look honey; I'll just stay as long as is decent here. There may be things to sort out, wills and that, but that's of no concern to me so

I'll leave them to it. Day or two maybe but I'll be home soon.

PJ and Seamie enter during following dialogue. Funeral clothes. Black ties. Seamie goes to bedroom, down stage right. PJ sits.

Sure, baby, missing you too. Give my guys a hug from me. Tell Shaun I may miss his football practice this week but I'll make it up next week. If he needs an auto to get there, tell him have mine. And ask Patrick to check if that motor for the cruiser came into stock in Wall Mart. Yeah, I'll call you tomorrow. A M. Yeah. 'Bye.

He sits at fire.

EAMONN	Big turn out.
PJ	What?
EAMONN	Big funeral. A lot of people. More than I would have expected.
PJ	Well, he was a good man for going to funerals himself. As long as he was able.
EAMONN	Yeah?
PJ	I think he thought he was still ahead of the posse, like. At a funeral. He was still to be had while another cowpoke bit the dust.
EAMONN	In the States, funerals work the other way. They're very private and you wouldn't go unless you felt you were invited.
PJ	Invited?
EAMONN	Yeah, you know someone would say to you 'Dad has passed on and I'd like you to come to the funeral.'
PJ	Even to an Irish funeral?
EAMONN	Well, I wouldn't know. There are no Irish around where I live.
PJ	Californighaa. I thought two of Peetie Henry's bucks were in California. Los Angeles. Is that not in California?
EAMONN	Yeah, it is. But I live in Sonora. In the wine valley. So you wouldn't meet too many Irish in the wine valley. At least, I wouldn't be looking for them.

PJ	It must be a mighty country.
EAMONN	Well, compared to this one, yes, it is.
PJ	What about Hollywood? Ha?
EAMONN	Hollywood isn't America.
PJ	Of course it is. Isn't it outside Los Angeles?
EAMONN	Physically, yes. What I mean is that Hollywood is Dreamland. It's not real. It could be anywhere. You know, there are very few films actually made in Hollywood any more.
PJ	Oh, I know, sure nearly all of Clint Eastwood's were made in Italy and Spain.
	Pause
	What's Sonora like?
EAMONN	Very nice. Warm. Nice people. Good civic pride.
PJ	Civic pride? What's that?
EAMONN	Well, it means they care for where they come from. Where they live. They mind it. Make sure it's not destroyed.
PJ	Oh, we have plenty of know alls to do that for us here. If we let them.
EAMONN	Yeah?
PJ	You don't leave too much value on where you come from when you never came back to it.
EAMONN	Now, PJ, you know that wasn't on. I couldn't afford to get sucked into whatever was going on here. And anyway, the option to leave was there for everyone.
PJ	I suppose.
EAMONN	You watch a lot of movies?
PJ	What?
EAMONN	*(at television)* You have quite a collection of videos.
PJ	Arrah, there was an auld video shop closing down in town and he had hundreds of them out the back. I gave him a ton for the whole lot. We're getting through them.
EAMONN	Did you get good value?
PJ	Well, there's a good few cowboys in it. Fair few Carry Ons as well.

EAMONN	Carry Ons?
PJ	They're auld English comedies. Good craic.
EAMONN	Any documentaries?
PJ	Documentaries?
EAMONN	Yes. National Geographic. They're terrific. Very detailed. Educational.
PJ	What are they about?
EAMONN	Oh, wildlife. You know.
PJ	Wildlife?
EAMONN	Yeah.
PJ	We see enough wildlife here without having to look at it on a video.
	Seamie enters in work clothes and heads for exit.
	Where are you off to?
SEAMIE	Graveyard.
PJ	For what?
SEAMIE	Fill.
PJ	Sure Flynn's men will do that. Aren't they paid to do it?
SEAMIE	Aye.
PJ	So what are you going down for?
SEAMIE	Just.
PJ	Your father is dead. Do you not know that? We buried him this morning.
SEAMIE	Aye.
PJ	So what's with the wan word now? It's over. Can you not talk right? Like a Christian.
EAMONN	You haven't forgotten how to talk, have you, Seamus?
SEAMIE	No.
EAMONN	That's good. Well, you take your time.
SEAMIE	Aye.
EAMONN	When you're good and ready, you'll begin again. Won't you?
SEAMIE	Yeah.
PJ	When will that be?
SEAMIE	*(shrugs)*
	Sometime.
PJ	When? What time?
SEAMIE	Eventually.

EAMONN	Leave him be, PJ. If he doesn't want to expand, let him be.
PJ	Go on outa my sight. Bejaysus, you're a twin for what's gone.
SEAMIE	Right.
	He exits.
PJ	You could get your National Geographic to come and make a documentary on that piece of wildlife. Whiskey?
EAMONN	Ah, why not?
	Pause
	Seamie is fairly traumatised by what happened.
PJ	Traumatised?
EAMONN	In shock. You know. Or whatever.
PJ	Well, now, you'd think he'd be out of it after twenty five years. That's pure thickness.
EAMONN	I'm not so sure. I was speaking to a psychiatrist at a party one night and I was telling him about Seamus and he suggested it would take an experience of similar magnitude to make him talk again.
PJ	What are you saying? That I should beat the shite out of him?
EAMONN	No. No. Not at all. It can be any kind of experience, any kind of danger that would affect him the same way.
PJ	And who told you this?
EAMONN	A psychiatrist.
PJ	Be God. I heard The Master saying one night that anyone that'd go to a psychiatrist would want to have their head examined.
	Pause
	I don't know what's going to become of that fella.
EAMONN	Why? How do you mean, become of him?
PJ	Well, he can hardly stay here, can he? It wouldn't be fair, would it?
EAMONN	Why not? It's his home, isn't it?
PJ	Yeah, but after.
EAMONN	After what?

PJ	When the place is mine and Mary and myself get married, sure he'll have to go somewhere. It wouldn't be fair on Mary, would it, to have him loping round the place as much use as a one legged man in an arse kicking competition.
EAMONN	Is the place yours?
PJ	Who the hell else is going to get it? It's hardly going to be left to a fella that absconded in middle of the night and never came back or to another bollocks that won't talk to anyone, beyond the wan word. Hah?
EAMONN	I suppose. Did he leave a will?
PJ	He did. It's within in Mr. Burke's office. He was very particular about things like that.
EAMONN	So, when is it going to be opened? Read?
PJ	Ah, you don't like doing things like that until after the Month's Mind. I'd say that's what the other buck is thinking, too.
EAMONN	How?
PJ	About the talk. He won't burst until after the Month's Mind.
EAMONN	And how long have yourself and Mary been engaged? I didn't know about that.
PJ	Engaged?
EAMONN	Yeah. When did you decide to get married? When did you propose?
PJ	Ah, Christ, there's nothing like that. It's just an understanding.
EAMONN	An understanding?
PJ	Yeah.
EAMONN	But how long are you dating?
PJ	Dating?
EAMONN	Yeah. Dating. Going out together.
PJ	Arrah, God help your wit. Isn't Mary up here ten times a day and me below as often? What need have we of dating?
EAMONN	But you have discussed marriage?
PJ	How do you mean?
EAMONN	Well, have you actually asked her to marry you and has

	she said yes?
PJ	What use would that be until we were in a position to do something about it? Christ, sure it was like The Usual Suspects in this house. How could we marry and me here like Kobayashi with Keyser Soze above shouting in the bed and Verbal Kint, the Man with the Plan, below in the other room sulking this past twenty five years. Anyway, her mother isn't too well either and now, I suppose, we'll have to wait for her to go to the worm factory.
EAMONN	I'm going down to see her this evening. I know she'd have been at the funeral if she wasn't so ill.
PJ	Ah, you'll hardly know her. She's fighting in the featherweight division now.
EAMONN	A truly great woman. I owe her; we all owe her a lot.
PJ	A good neighbour. And that's another reason why I'll be glad that Mary and myself will be here to keep the thing going, like. There's only a few of us left.
EAMONN	I didn't realise Corky had died. How long is he dead for?
PJ	For good.
	They laugh.
EAMONN	You know what I mean.
PJ	Aye. About twelve months. Had a tough session with it too. It was the only bit of hard work he ever did in his life.
EAMONN	What he die from?
PJ	Oh, the galloping gourmet.
EAMONN	What?
PJ	Cancer.
EAMONN	Who's in the place now?
PJ	No one. She's for sale. The lads are in Manchester and the daughter is working in the multi-story school in Carrick.
EAMONN	So, Seamie is going to go.
PJ	He'll have to.
EAMONN	Go where?
PJ	I don't know. California.

EAMONN	I don't think Seamie would hack it in America.
PJ	Neither do I. Seamie is built more for comfort than speed.
EAMONN	Maybe he'll get married now, as well.
PJ	Wan Word?
EAMONN	Yeah. Why not? I can see it happening.
PJ	You have as much chance of seeing shite coming out of a rocking horse.
EAMONN	Well, you're going to look after yourself, anyway.
PJ	Look, Yank, you can write that down in block capitals. I've lived in this place for nearly fifty years. And what have I to show for it. Trying to squeeze a living out of the land and every smart Alec in Dublin and Brussels telling you to give it back to the snipe and the fox. Putting up with two lunatics for the past twenty-five years, one of them madder than the other. Living in an asylum isn't a great place to be if you're trying to stay sane. It's an awful way to be if all that's keeping you alive is the thought of your father dying. I never had a day's luck in my life. If I bought a graveyard, people would stop dying. But I have the ball at my feet at last and I'm going to make hay from here on in.
EAMONN	Did the old man know about you and Mary?
PJ	We never spoke of it. He wouldn't have approved. And he spent most of his time trying to marry me off to a niece of Corky's.
EAMONN	Yeah?
PJ	She was nursing in Dublin. She'd come down here on the prowl. Wouldn't you think she'd get something about Dublin with all that's there in all colours and creeds. But, Jesus, if you saw her. The tide wouldn't take her out.
EAMONN	Yeah? That bad?
PJ	Well, she wouldn't be heading for Tralee in August and that's for sure. But I had to fend that off as well as everything else. And do you know what I was thinking last night?
	(rummaging in drawer)

Do you know what I have to show for near sixty years on this earth? What recognition I got? A county junior football medal and a medal for sean-nos singing at a County Fleadh. And do you know what? They're two runners-up medals. So, now, boy, I've decided. I'm finished with being runner-up. When the will is done and the time is right, I'll sit down with Mary and I'll do and say whatever has to be done and said to marry her. Wan Word can have the road and I don't give two fucks what happens to him. He can ride off into the sunset like Shane in the movie for all I care because I'm going into the winner's enclosure in the end. So, you see, a watched kettle does boil and there'll be no more runners-up medals for PJ.

EAMONN	Fair enough.
PJ	Will I fill that again?
EAMONN	Just top it up.

Pause

You know, the last time I drank a Power's Whiskey was the night before I left. Twenty five years ago. Down in Mary's. I remember her mother pouring it.

PJ	What were you doing down there that night?
EAMONN	Why not?
PJ	That night? The night of the beating?
EAMONN	Yeah. Looking for sanctuary, I suppose. A safe house. I figured, being the middle son, I was next if it carried on, so I got out. I stayed there that night.
PJ	And left me next in line.
EAMONN	I knew you were able to handle yourself.
PJ	You know he never lifted a hand to man or beast after that night.
EAMONN	I didn't think he would.
PJ	Yeah?
EAMONN	What would you have done if he had?
PJ	I'd have levelled him.
EAMONN	See. I knew that.
PJ	So, why didn't you stay? Why did you go, if you knew that?

EAMONN	Ah, it was a chance. An excuse. The middle son of three only gets what drops off two other tables. You never have your own space. Do you know, the day I left here every stitch of clothes I had on me had been worn by you. And if I'd stayed would I not be riding off into the sunset with Seamie, now.
PJ	I suppose. Maybe. Anyway, it worked out well for you.
EAMONN	Yeah, I came pretty good.
PJ	The lads are well?
EAMONN	Yeah, fine. Both in college. On break at the moment. Doing good.
PJ	And herself?
EAMONN	She's fine. Yeah, Carol's just fine.
PJ	You know, now that it's over and all, you should come for a holiday. Show the lads where they spring from. Show the wife Ireland.
EAMONN	Maybe, yeah, maybe someday I might do that.
PJ	Tell you what. Come for the wedding. You could give Mary away.
EAMONN	I could give Mary away? How could I do that? I couldn't do that.
PJ	Why not?
EAMONN	How could one brother give away a woman to another brother?
PJ	I don't see why not. She'll hardly have her father to do it.
EAMONN	Any word from him? Has he ever been back?
PJ	Never. I think he rings the odd time.
EAMONN	Where is he?
PJ	I don't know. Italy or Turkey or someplace. Wherever the circus is.
EAMONN	Strange thing.
PJ	What?
EAMONN	That happening. Mary's mother was brave to do what she did at the time.
PJ	What?
EAMONN	To keep the child. Very brave.
PJ	Well, if the world was fair there'd be no need for

	bravery.
EAMONN	Yeah. I suppose.
PJ	Well, there weren't many that wanted her to keep it. And the Circus Man was gone. They say Mary was three or four before he knew anything about her. And it can't have been easy with the Canon on the job and all. But she held firm. And she has Mary to show for it.
EAMONN	God, she had a tough life. Bringing up a child with no help from Church or State.
PJ	Well, she was never beat, before or since. An independent lady.
EAMONN	And now she has a daughter to pay her back for all she's done.
	Pause
PJ	Can I ask you something?
EAMONN	Sure, shoot.
PJ	If Wan Word was to ask you to take him to America, would you?
EAMONN	Well, I sure as hell can't stop him coming to America, but he ain't coming near me.
PJ	No?
EAMONN	No way, Jose. You think I should?
PJ	He's your brother.
EAMONN	PJ, I think we'd better get this family shit sorted out so as there's no confusion. I bailed out of here twenty five years ago and I only came back to bury this guy. To make sure he was dead, if you like. That's it. End of story. I have a family of my own now. In Sonora, California and it don't include either of you two dudes. Ok, it's good to see you again and it's nice to keep in touch. That's fine. But if I don't see either of you for another twenty five years, that's fine too. See, I have a life. A real life. Not Hollywood. Reality. And there is no room in that life for a brother who has all the plans made to marry a woman whom he hasn't even taken on a date nor another one who's gone to fill in his father's grave so that he can dance on it afterwards. Got it? Or as your film friend Joe Peschi might say 'capiche?'

PJ	Capiche
	Mary rushes in, distressed.
MARY	Where's Wan Word.
PJ	He's in the graveyard. Filling in Daddy. Why?
MARY	Can you come down? Quick.
EAMONN	Mary, what's wrong?
MARY	It's Mammy.
PJ	What about her?
MARY	She's dead.

BLACK OUT

END OF ACT ONE

INTERVAL

ACT TWO

SCENE ONE

One week later. Eamonn is preparing to return to America. Suitcase on floor. He is looking through videos.
Mary enters.

EAMONN	Oh, hi, Mary.
MARY	Eamonn.
EAMONN	Jeez, these guys have some collection of videos.
MARY	PJ nearly knows them all off by heart.
EAMONN	He was telling me how he came by them. The store closing.
MARY	What store?
EAMONN	Some place in town. The guy sold the stock cheap.
MARY	Not at all. He got stuck in some mail order yoke years ago and they keep sending him videos. He can't get them stopped. They'd have him cleaned if he paid them. There's some mistake in the system. He keeps getting videos but he never gets a bill. Then when the other buck used go up the North he'd bring back a rake of blue ones.
EAMONN	What other buck?
MARY	Wan Word.
EAMONN	What would take him up the North?
MARY	He used drive an odd load of sheep up for Dodger Duignan. The Dodger used bring them back and forth and draw subsidies on both sides of the border. Willie the butcher says you'd always know one of The Dodger's sheep for he'd have a reel in his head from going around in circles. But Franz Fischler finished all that with his one cheque.
EAMONN	Who?

117

MARY	Ah, the Common Market. New rules.
EAMONN	And he'd bring back adult movies?
MARY	Aye. You could nearly see steam coming out the chimney here the night he'd come back.

Pause

So, you're off the day?

EAMONN	Yeah, this afternoon. Train to Dublin, overnight there and back in the morning.
MARY	Eamonn, it was very good of you to stay for my mother's funeral.
EAMONN	It was the least I could do. I don't forget, Mary. I doubt if we could have survived without your mother. And the time of the bust up between Seamie and our father, she was all I had to turn to. Her and you. Here, I just boiled the kettle, fancy a tea or coffee or something stronger.
MARY	What are you having?
EAMONN	Well, I bought a jar of coffee the other day and I doubt if these two guys will use it.
MARY	Make me a cup, so. I'll chance it. See how the Yanks make it.
EAMONN	It's instant.
MARY	Everything in America is.
EAMONN	*(laughing)*

I suppose it seems that way.

Pause

She got a good send off.

MARY	Yeah. She'd have enjoyed seeing the crowd. Although, some of them she'd have wondered about. 'What the hell is he looking for, coming to my funeral? Gawkin.'
EAMONN	Yeah? I wouldn't know hardly anyone there except a few that came to introduce themselves. This young guy came over and said 'You won't know me, Eamonn, but I'm James Green, the local TD.' And before I could help myself I asked him was he The Weasel's son. I don't think he was too pleased.
MARY	No, That boy wouldn't want to be known as The Weasel's son.

EAMONN	How did he manage to become a TD?
MARY	Oh, God knows. How did Bush come to be President? The Master says 'Weasel Óg was elected by the significant number of sane constituents who refused to vote for any candidate.' I suppose he was the best of a bad lot.
EAMONN	And they're still going to funerals. The politicians.
MARY	Still running through graveyards after the live vote. And half the time they don't even know who's dead. Only they're told to go. **She laughs.**
EAMONN	What's so funny?
MARY	Do you remember the Pelter McGowan beyond in Killowen.
EAMONN	Yeah. Gee, he was one cranky man.
MARY	One? If cranky men were scarce he make three or four of them. Talk about this house. This place was a haven of peace and serenity compared with The Pelter's. Morning, noon and night, grumbling about everything, fighting with the sons. They could do nothing right. Two saints they were, to stick it. Anyway, he died and Greene the TD, that you met the day, arrived at the funeral. And the funeral was more like a carnival, the lads were so glad to get rid of The Pelter. And the TD goes over with this long face to one of the sons and after sympathising, he says 'how old was your father'? 'Eighty three' says Markeen, the son. 'And,' says Green, 'I didn't hear he was sick, was he long complaining'? 'Eighty three fuckin' years' sez Markeen. **They laugh.**
EAMONN	God, The Pelter was some detail. **Pause** Are you lonely, Mary?
MARY	Well, I don't know what way I am, to tell you the truth. I knew she was dying. Of course I did and I had myself well geared for that but I didn't know how big a hole would be left when she went. You know, I turn to say something to her a hundred times a day. I think she

	should still be in the corner. I don't know how to fill the day yet. So much of the day involved taking care of her,
EAMONN	Boy, you took some care of her alright. You should be very proud. Besides the set-up here with my father.
MARY	Ah that was different, Eamonn. Men aren't built for looking after the sick. They haven't the patience. And then there was all the auld shite with Wan Word and himself and poor PJ got caught fool in the middle of the whole lot. Is it any wonder there was more relief than sorrow after the old man died?
EAMONN	Yeah, I suppose. I'm just thinking, these days seeing your mother's death and the way she was mourned, we should have done more in this house to heal things. Now, it's too late.
MARY	It's only natural to think that way after a death, Eamonn. You always regret not saying things or doing things. No matter how hard or how well you tried to do things, you always feel some guilt.
EAMONN	I cried at your mother's funeral. I observed my father's. She was like our mother after Mammy died. Sure who reared Seamus? Wasn't she up here every day until he went to school? Didn't she make sure we were all kitted out right wherever we went?
MARY	She always said she was only giving back what she got. The time she had the trouble, your Mammy was the only one that stood with her. Apart from her own parents, of course, and sure God love them; they had to sway with the Church.
EAMONN	The time she had the trouble. God, what sort of people were we that could describe bringing a child into the world as 'being in trouble'? Was it the Church that taught us language like that?
MARY	That was the way it was, Eamonn. The times that were in it. No use shouting back at them now. My mother had to walk a rough road but she never complained. She said to me one time that the two things that could never be taken from her were her daughter and the

	Circus Man.
EAMONN	She loved him.
MARY	'Till she drew her last breath.
EAMONN	Wasn't it a pity that the love of such a great woman should be wasted on a man like that.
MARY	It wasn't, Eamonn. It wasn't wasted. He loved her, too. In whatever way he could. Daddy couldn't stay. Even if he wanted to. I like to think he did. Want to. But the travel is in the Circus Man's blood. Now the poor man is hobbled like the rest of us. Imagine a tight-rope walker crippled with arthritis. Imprisoned.
EAMONN	Does he know your mother died?
MARY	Oh, aye. I rang him. He lives in a little village outside a place called Verona, in Italy. He has three sons. His wife knows about me but the sons don't so we have to be careful and I only ring when I know the sons are on the road with the circus. He cried when I told him. You could tell he was upset. I felt sorry for him but I was glad he cried.
EAMONN	Glad?
MARY	For Mammy. It said what she meant to him.
EAMONN	Did you never want to see him?
MARY	Oh God, I did. For a long time I was obsessed. Nearly demanding.
EAMONN	Why didn't you? Why don't you? Go see him, like.
	Pause
MARY	Three was a three-ring circus in Sligo one time. I didn't know it was on or anything but I went in on the bus with Mammy. She was getting new glasses. And didn't she spot the poster for the circus in the ESB window. If you saw her face. She was twenty again. And there was a matinee so we said we'd go and get the evening bus home. So there's the pair of us within at the circus in the middle of a crowd of screeching children. Candy floss, clowns dolls pissing on us, cars exploding, the whole works. And she's having the time of her life. And the tears are running down her face and I don't know is it with joy or sorrow. And there's two high wire

walkers in two of the rings. That was one of Daddy's jobs. And one of them has a safety net and the other hasn't. And Mammy says to me 'Mary, look at them two bucks and tell me which do you think is more likely to fall'? And I said the one with the safety net and she said 'Mary, your father never walked with a safety net and don't you ever be bothered with a man with a safety net for you'll spend your life lifting him out of it after he falls.' After that I couldn't go to meet Daddy.

EAMONN   Why not?

MARY   She had painted such a picture of the man. This fearless giant. I was afraid I'd be disappointed.

EAMONN   Is that why you wouldn't come with me that time?

MARY   What?

EAMONN   When I was going to America. You wouldn't come. Were you afraid you'd be disappointed?

MARY   No, Eamonn. I knew I wouldn't be disappointed. But I had a duty to my mother. I couldn't leave her.

EAMONN   But she told you to go with me. She encouraged you.

MARY   What else would you expect her to do? But when they came to her, when she was carrying me, with the address in London where she should go to get rid of me, she didn't abandon me. So I wouldn't desert her, no matter what she said. But I knew I wouldn't be disappointed, Eamonn, and I cried many's a bitter tear after you.

EAMONN   I should have made you come with me.

         Pause

         I loved you

MARY   Arrah shut up that auld nonsense, Eamonn. What would you have been doing with a yoke like me? I'm afraid when I was being assembled God was on his lunch break. I wouldn't have gone. Couldn't have gone. One Circus Man was enough in our house. Anyway, it worked out the best for you. If I went would you ever have got to California? Met Carol?

EAMONN   California was an accident. I was just asked to drive a

	load over there from work and was offered a full time
	job there. I liked the sun so I said yeah. Carol ran the
	office there and that's how we met. The rest is history.
MARY	So it was all accidental.
EAMONN	Yeah.
MARY	You really believe that, don't you?
EAMONN	Yeah, why shouldn't I?
	Pause
MARY	Did you love Carol when you married her?
EAMONN	What? What do you mean?
MARY	Did you?
	Pause
EAMONN	Well, I don't know. I certainly thought I did, otherwise
	I wouldn't have married her. But if you mean I married
	her on some sort of rebound, maybe I did. Maybe.
	I didn't want to be alone, Mary. I didn't want to be
	alone.
MARY	Do you love her now?
EAMONN	Yes, I do. But is it not possible to love two people?
MARY	We had our time. We were lucky that nobody knew
	or found out because then we'd have been forced into
	something we might have regretted.
EAMONN	I wouldn't.
MARY	Stick with the memory, Eamonn. Stick with the
	memory.
	Pause
	You know your father always wanted to meet Carol.
EAMONN	Yeah?
MARY	He felt you were taking revenge on him, not bringing
	her to meet him.
EAMONN	It wasn't that. That wasn't it.
MARY	Then what?
EAMONN	Look, Mary, I felt I owed it to you not to bring her.
	Not to cast her up before you saying this is the woman
	I chose above you. Because that wasn't the way it was.
	And...
MARY	And?
EAMONN	I have a good life. A good life with Carol. But I was

	afraid if I brought her here, I might begin to compare her to you and she might come off worst. I had that to lose, Mary, can you see that?
MARY	Strange, I'd never have thought of you as a safety net man.
EAMONN	Well, whatever. So it was as well that only the three of us knew.
MARY	Four. Four of us.
EAMONN	Four?
MARY	Your father knew.
EAMONN	How? It was hardly your mother who told him.
MARY	No. Fathers just know things like that. He never said a word until the last week he was alive. He said you'd be coming for the funeral but I couldn't go with you this time either because you were married.
EAMONN	God. Well at least he met my boys.

Pause

MARY	Eamonn, how did you know that?
EAMONN	What?
MARY	That the boys were here.
EAMONN	It's like you say, fathers know these things. Naw, they told their mother and she thought I should know.
MARY	Did you go ape?
EAMONN	*(laughing)*

No, I saw enough of that here. No, they're good guys and if it was something they wanted to do, let them do it. As long as they didn't involve me in it.

MARY	Why? Why did you never want to bring your family here? Just the boys, even. On a holiday. It's where you come from. Are you that ashamed of it?
EAMONN	Ashamed? I don't know. No, I don't think that's the right word. For as long as I could remember I wanted to be somewhere else. I knew I wanted to get away from here. And the beating, the row with Seamus, gave me the excuse. So then I went to ask you to come with me and when that didn't work out, your mother made me stay the night. Remember? In the morning she brought me into town, got a loan for my airfare

and one hundred dollars out of the bank. She said the money was so I wouldn't have to lift the first shovel I saw. She put me on the Dublin bus and said 'off with you now, Eamonn and join the circus. Mary and you are not meant to be.'

(chuckling)

I remember when I asked her how she was able to borrow the money she said 'arrah, that auld eejit of a bank manager has a notion of me.' What a woman. I paid it back inside a year.

MARY   I never knew that. That she did that.

EAMONN   Well she did. And after that, I'm expected to come back and make speeches about the misty green isle and how horrible it is to be separated from the land of my birth. Bullshit.

Pause

And anyway, the place I left no longer exists. God, look at Carrick now. A multi-story school.

MARY   Where?

EAMONN   In Carrick. PJ said Corky's daughter was teaching in a multi-story school in Carrick.

MARY   A Montessori school. Multi-story. Jesus, PJ is some eejit.

EAMONN   You think?

MARY   Yeah.

EAMONN   Anyway, that was your mother. Only for her I'd never have got away.

MARY   Sometimes, she said only for her you'd never have had to go away.

EAMONN   Why? What did she mean?

MARY   Well the incident that led to the beating.

EAMONN   What actually happened that evening, Mary? What started it? I never knew. Did she ever say? I saw your mother leave the house here but I only came in when I heard the screaming.

MARY   He wanted to marry my mother. Your father. She never encouraged him or anything but he kept at her. Coddin' at first, like, but then it got serious. And that evening

	it got very serious. She told him to have sense, that she had no intention of marrying him. Then he said 'if I was a tramp out of a circus, you'd be free enough with me.' She said nothing, just walked out the door and never stood in the house again. Seamie was there, took on his father about what he said and you know what happened after that.
EAMONN	Christ.
MARY	And she wouldn't die before him. I often heard her praying to God to spare her until after he was gone. It was an eye for an eye and that left both of them half-blind.
EAMONN	Well, she got her wish.
MARY	She got her wish and now they're both gone and we're all left with one arm as long as the other.
EAMONN	Well, at least you have PJ.
MARY	PJ?
EAMONN	Yeah. You have that to look forward to.
MARY	What?
EAMONN	Getting married. You know. Moving in here.
MARY	Getting married? To PJ?
EAMONN	Yeah.
MARY	You're joking me. Who said that?
EAMONN	PJ.
MARY	PJ? Where did he get that notion?
EAMONN	I don't know. But he's fairly certain that it's the plan. Now that the old pair are gone. Is it not? Are you not marrying PJ?
MARY	Jesus Christ, Eamonn, I couldn't marry PJ.
EAMONN	Why not?
MARY	Why not? I don't know. Arrah, I couldn't. Sure PJ is a friend of mine.
EAMONN	And can friends not get married?
MARY	There was many's a great friendship ruined by marriage. Mammy told me the Circus Man said marriage was a powerful cure for love. But you know what I mean. I'd have to be in love to get married. PJ? Oh God, no. Sure if I married PJ I'd know everyday

	what was going to happen tomorrow. What craic would there be in that? No, if I was getting married it would have to be to some unpredictable get like my father. Or you.
EAMONN	Or Seamie
MARY	Or Wan Word. Now there's a boy with no safety net.
EAMONN	Would you marry Seamie?
MARY	Sure Seamie can't get married.
EAMONN	Why not?
MARY	Isn't 'I do' two words. He couldn't say it.
	They laugh.
EAMONN	He'll come out of that.
MARY	He will. When it suits him. Or when he knows he has to, to get something he wants badly. There's one thing sure, whenever he bursts, it'll be worth hearing. He's a tough tulip, Wan Word. But PJ? And he thinks I'm going to marry him? God, what am I going to do about this?
EAMONN	Be careful now. This is like my father and your mother. Don't encourage him.
MARY	I never encouraged him. Anytime he ever mentioned stuff like that I'd change the subject.
EAMONN	Mary, let him down easy. He deserves that much.
MARY	He'll be alright. He'll recover. PJ'll find someone to take him out of the safety net after the fall.
	PJ enters.
PJ	We'd better hightail it, Eamonn, that train is at half past. Will you come with us for the spin, Mary?
MARY	I'll stay here and clean up a bit. Where's Wan Word.
PJ	He's in the car. Listening to Garth Brooks.
EAMONN	I've got friends in low places.
PJ	I've got friends in no places would be more like it with that buck. Anyway, have you everything with you?
EAMONN	Yeah, I think so.
	(glancing at Mary)
	At least everything that I can bring with me. Anyway, I'm better prepared than the last time I left.
MARY	Well, don't be so long away this time and don't be

	waiting for one of us to die to come home.
EAMONN	No, I won't.
PJ	Think about what we were talking about. You'll come home to do that wee job for us. We'd appreciate it.
	(lifting case)
	I'll put this in the boot
	He exits.
MARY	What wee job?
EAMONN	He wants me to give you away at the wedding.
MARY	Oh, God, no.
EAMONN	*(at door)*
	So remember what I said. Be careful.
	He kisses her on the cheek and exits.
	She stands in doorway touching her face where she has been kissed.
	Sound of car starting and leaving yard.
	Mary returns and sits.
MARY	*(to herself)*
	I'll tell you one thing, Eamonn, if you had asked me to go with you this time, I would.

FADE DOWN

SCENE TWO

One month later. PJ is sitting reading letter aloud. Seamie is sorting and rewinding videos.

PJ   It was good to see you guys again and see that you
            are making out ok. It was also good to see Mary and
            be able to stay for her mother's funeral. That woman
            was real good to all of us. I'd like to think that you
            guys would take care of Mary now. She may not be as
            strong as she pretends to be. Anyway, I'll keep in touch
            and give me a bell if you ever need anything. Yours
            sincerely, Ed.
            Ed. Bejaysus, he couldn't even bring his own name out
            of the place. What?

SEAMIE   Aye.

PJ   Take care of Mary. Well, don't worry, Mary will be
            taken care of. Have you any notion what you're going
            to do yet?

SEAMIE   How?

PJ   When Mary moves in here.

SEAMIE   Aye.

PJ   Well, what?

SEAMIE   What?

PJ   What are you going to do?

            Seamie shrugs.

            Well, you'd better put your thinking cap on. Because
            you can't stay here. There's going to be no cosy cartel
            in this house. This isn't The Little House on the Prairie
            or The Waltons. None of your 'night Paw, 'night
            John Boy craic here. We'll go into Mr. Burke's office
            tomorrow and have the will read and we'll see if he left
            any few pound as well as the place. If he did, you're
            welcome to that. If he didn't, Mary and myself will
            see you alright and you leaving. We're not animals
            altogether. But leave you must. This isn't Friends or

Frazier where all live on top of one another. When a
man and a woman get married, they need to be on their
own. There's things they might like to be at, any hour
of the day or night and they wouldn't want a gobshite
pounding about the place, watching videos at all hours,
and yahooing at Angelina Jolie or Nicole Kidman.
Capiche?

SEAMIE   Capiche.

PJ   So, ponder your position. PJ has his sentence served
this past twenty five years with the pair of ye. Jesus,
the Guildford Four only did sixteen years and I was as
innocent as them. But now, The Eagle has landed and
it's time to start living in earnest. Ferris Buller's Day
Off won't be a patch on PJ's.

SEAMIE   Right.

Mary enters.

MARY   There you are lads. There's an auld soda farl for ye. My
eye was bigger than my stomach when I was baking it
and I forgot about Mammy being gone. How are ye the
day?

SEAMIE   Bully.

PJ   Not too bad. We got a letter from Eamonn, or should I
say Ed.

MARY   Mr. Ed.

PJ   Be God, aye. Do you remember? The Talking Horse.

MARY   Is he well?

PJ   Well, we have to have it translated into English but I
think there's no loss on him.

MARY   It was nice to see him again. He changed a fair bit but
sure, I suppose, we hardly stood still ourselves.

SEAMIE   Hardly.

MARY   No sign of you bursting into song yet, Wan Word?

SEAMIE   No.

PJ   I thought when the Month's Mind was done, he'd climb
down and rejoin the human race but you might as well
be trying to get Paisley to say Mass. Maybe tomorrow,
when the will is read, he might explode.

MARY   Are ye going in tomorrow?

SEAMIE	Aye.
MARY	Morning?
SEAMIE	Eleven.
PJ	Then the die will be cast. There'll be big changes then, Mary. What? What way does the old paper ad put it? Questions answered and answers questioned. There's good times ahead.
MARY	Maybe. We'll see.
PJ	No maybe about it. Life is only starting.
MARY	Wan Word?
SEAMIE	What?
MARY	Have you nothing to say about this?
SEAMIE	Wait.
PJ	Wait? Oh, you can wait as long as you like. I told him already, Mary, he can start doing like the Palestinians on the West Bank, start preparing for a strategic withdrawal.
	Pause
	Is there anything needs doing down there?
MARY	No. Sure I'm well fit now on my own when I don't have Mammy to look after. It fills the day having the outside work.
PJ	And the nights?
MARY	Ah, the nights are lonesome. We used to have great nights together, herself and myself. I was never outside Ireland and still I've seen the world. She brought me to all the cities and countries the Circus Man told her about. 'Look up, the weather in the paper' she'd say 'and see if there's any place you'd like to go tonight.' And I'd look and maybe say it's nice in Belgium, Mammy. Take me to Belgium. 'Belgium' she'd say, 'Brussels, Liege and Bruges. Ah, Mary, wait 'till you see Bruges.' And she'd take me on an escorted tour of Belgium.
	Pause
	I miss her. I miss the two of them at night. Mammy and the Circus Man.
	Pause

	Anyway, I'd better be going back. There's a clocking hen to be minded. I'll see you later.
PJ	Right, Mary. I'll call down later for a chat.
SEAMIE	Mary.
MARY	Yes, Wan Word.
SEAMIE	Pictures?
MARY	Pictures?
SEAMIE	Tonight.
MARY	What? Is the mobile cinema around?
SEAMIE	Aye.
MARY	What's on?
SEAMIE	Unforgiven.
PJ	Clint Eastwood.
MARY	Any good?
PJ	1992. Nine academy nominations. Four wins. Best picture, Clint for best director, Gene Hackman for best supporting actor and Joel Cox for best film editing. Clint was beaten for best actor by Al Pacino for Scent of a Woman and it was the year that Neil Jordan won best screenplay for The Crying Game. It grossed over 150 million dollars in America alone.
MARY	What is it about?
PJ	Well you see...
SEAMIE	*(interrupting)* There's this small town in The Wild West called Big Whiskey. And there's a saloon in the town with a brothel in it. And these two cowboys are in the brothel one night, a young fella and an older dude. And the older fella is with this young wan who's only new to the game and knows feck all. And when your man strips off, she sees he has a fierce small apparatus. And she starts giggling. Now, you should never laugh at a man's mickey, even if it was only the size of PJ's there. And your man took the hump and he got the young fella to hold her and he went at her with a knife. Destroyed her. And the sheriff is sent for and he arrives on the scene. But who is it only Gene Hackman and you know bloody well that your woman will get

nowhere with Hackman. If she was going to, Hackman wouldn't be playing the part. It would be James Garner or some auld softie like that. So Hackman tells the pair of boys to bring in a few horses to the woman by the end of the month and to fuck off out of the place in the meantime. What good a few horses are going to be to the wan with the flittered face is a thing that's never fully explained and you could say, if you wanted to be critical, that it's a weakness in the script. Anyway, all the women in the flop house pool their money and decide to put the word out that they'll pay a thousand dollars to anyone that'll kill the pair of bucks. A thousand is a fair auld bit of money at that time. Remember, now, we're talking about a place that has no headage or ewe premiums. And the word spreads and, of course, Gene Hackman gets to hear about it and he lets it be known that he'll sort out anyone that comes to town, looking to collect. There's this young fella up north and he fancies a crack at the reward but he's cute enough to know he mightn't be able to do it on his own so, on the way down, he calls on Clint Eastwood. Clint hung up his guns years ago and got married. He was a pig farmer though, looking at the set up he had, I doubt if any of them ever made a Donnelly sausage. Anyway, his wife was dead and he was rearing a young son and daughter in the middle of the pigs. The young fella laid the proposal on Clint but Clint more or less told him to fuck off, that he was finished with that game and the young fella left. After he was gone, Clint fell on his face into the pig shit, trying to catch a sow. And when he saw the state of himself he must have said 'arrah, fuck this for a game of soldiers, I'm off to make some easy money.' So he tells the pair of youngsters what to do and heads off across the river to pick up an old mate who is also retired. Who is it only Morgan Freeman. Now, if you are in any doubt about the film up to this, you can cast it aside because once you see Morgan Freeman you know it's going to be good because Morgan Freeman was never in a bad film in his life. They say he's the best black actor since Sidney Poitier but I think he's better. Did you ever see Seven? Or The Shawshank Redemption? Mighty stuff. You see, I think the difference between Poitier and Freeman is that Freeman can play white parts, if you know what I mean. You never think of his colour when you're looking at a picture he's in. Of course, when Morgan hears the craic, he ups and leaves the wife, an Indian, mind you, nothing straightforward about Morgan Freeman, and heads off with Clint. They catch up with the young fella and agree a split on the reward. Be God, what do they discover the first night away but that the young buck has fierce bad lamps. Nearly as blind as a bat and as far as shooting is concerned he wouldn't hit a horse's hole with a hurley. So Clint and Morgan know they're probably going to do any shooting that's to be done but sure they're well used to that. So they head off for Big Whiskey. In the meantime, another buck arrives in Big Whiskey to go for the reward. A fella called English Bob and who do you think is playing him only Richard Harris from Limerick. This is a very flamboyant, flashy fucker who breezes into town with a reporter who is writing English Bob's life story, called the Duke of Death. When Hackman hears he is in town, he goes to meet him and makes fun of Harris, calling the book the Duck of Death and that. In the end, he disarms Harris and takes him out on the street and kicks seven different colours of shite out of him. Now, normally, I wouldn't be wild about Hackman cause there's usually no give at all in him but he goes up in my estimation for kicking Harris because he's only doing what the whole country would like to do. Because that Harris fella thought his shite was marmalade. Listening to him, you'd swear he was born in LA instead of Limerick, with the plummy voice. And Richard? When he left Limerick he was Dickey. A bit like our buck in California. Ed. Anyway, Harris, or what's left of him, is run out of town and that's the last of Harris, God rest him, I hope he's happy but he was an awful bollocks. When the three lads get into town, Clint is dosed with the cold and he waits in the saloon while the other pair check out the knocking shop upstairs. Hackman arrives and gives Clint an awful hiding. Did you ever notice that Clint Eastwood is a mighty man to take a beating? Anyway, the other two boys get out the window upstairs and take Clint off with them. In the run of a few days, he's suckin' diesel again and they go off to kill the two bucks. Begod, if poor auld Morgan Freeman can't pull the trigger. He's past it and Clint has to shoot the first fella for him. They decide to head for the Bar T ranch to kill the other fella but Morgan wants to go home. On the way, isn't the poor hoor captured and brought into Big Whiskey to Hackman and I don't have to tell you what he does to him, 'till in the end he dies and it's a blessed relief for the poor man. Anyway, Clint and the young fella wait outside the ranch-house until eventually your man has to come out to go to the jacks. Doesn't the young fella creep up and open the bog door and put three bullets in the buck. Caught with his trousers down, you might say. And he got that close that even he couldn't miss. Then they head back for Big Whiskey and wait outside the town for one of the women to come out with the money for the job. When she comes out, she tells them about Morgan Freeman being dead and Clint puts that puss on him, you know the one that tells you there's going to be a rake of men shot fairly soon. And that's what happens. He rides into town and shoots all hands. Gene Hackman and all. And then he goes home. So, will you come?

PJ   What need has she of seeing it now? Aren't you after telling all?

SEAMIE Will you?

MARY   *(dumbstruck)*
        That must have been what it was like when The Circus

	Man told Mammy things.
SEAMIE	Will you come?
MARY	I will. I will.
	(going to exit)
	Pick me up at seven.
	She exits.
	Pause
PJ	What the fuck do you think you're playing at?
SEAMIE	What?
PJ	You don't open your mouth for twenty five years, beyond the wan word and then you decide to cut loose and take my woman to the pictures.
SEAMIE	Your woman? Who said she was your woman?
PJ	I did.
SEAMIE	She didn't.
PJ	She doesn't need to. She knows. Everybody knows.
SEAMIE	So if she is, what harm is there in me taking her to the pictures.
PJ	You should have asked me.
SEAMIE	Asked you what?
PJ	If you could.
SEAMIE	If I could. The man that had that power is a month in the worm factory. And it wasn't as if you were going to take her. Were you?
PJ	All the same.
SEAMIE	All the same. The woman is lonely down there and you heard what Eamonn said in the letter. We have to look after her.
PJ	I suppose. But mind yourself now. No funny stuff. Remember your place. And your place isn't at the pictures with Mary. And you didn't even tell the story right.
SEAMIE	How?
PJ	You left out the bit about the flittered wan coming out to Clint when he was getting over the beating from Hackman and offering him a bit and him turning it down.
SEAMIE	I didn't want to be bringing too much sex into a story

	I'd be telling Mary.
PJ	All the same, it was important in the context of the film. It showed the kind a character Clint was. He'd shoot round him but he was still faithful to the wife even though she was dead.
SEAMIE	*(going to bedroom)* I'll get togged out. I'll be bringing the car.
PJ	I don't know is there much juice in that car. We need it to go to the solicitor in the morning.
SEAMIE	There's a two gallon tin in the barn. There always is. **He exits.**
PJ	Right. You have all the answers, smart boy. Only that I know how solid Mary is, feck the pictures you'd be at tonight because I wouldn't trust you as far as I throw you.

FADE DOWN

SCENE THREE

Later that night. PJ sits at table doing jigsaw. Behind him, on the TV, the film, The Cincinnati Kid is running. It is at the seminal scene (card game scene) in the film. PJ is shouting encouragement at Steve McQueen until Edward G Robinson reveals the Jack of Diamonds and the winning hand at which point PJ shouts 'shite, he had the Jack.' He switches off the television.

PJ   Fair play to you Edward G Robinson. That was a great piece of casting because you were the only one we would believe could ever get the better of Steve McQueen. Poor auld Steve, you had a sad end, too.

He begins to piece the jigsaw together. A car is heard to pull up and stop. Door closes. Back door opens and Seamie enters scullery.

SEAMIE   Hardy man.

PJ   Well.

SEAMIE   You're at the jigsaw.

PJ   Aye.

SEAMIE   How is it going?

PJ   Arrah, the sky is a hoor.

SEAMIE   Aye. Have you the edging done?

PJ   I have.

SEAMIE   Well then, leave the sky 'till last.

PJ   Are you going to start telling me how to do jigsaws now?

Pause

SEAMIE   Grand night out.

PJ   Was there many?

SEAMIE   About half full. Do you want anything?

PJ   What?

SEAMIE   Supper. Do you want anything?

PJ   No.

Seamie enters with large cheese sandwich and pint glass

	of milk. He sits at the fireside.
	Silence.
	Seamie begins to sing quietly.
	'And lay the blanket on the ground.'
PJ	Where were you?
SEAMIE	At the pictures.
PJ	The pictures are over hours ago.
SEAMIE	I know.
PJ	Where were you since?
SEAMIE	We went to Flynn's after.
PJ	Flynn's?
SEAMIE	The chipper.
	Silence.
	Seamie chuckles.
	PJ looks.
SEAMIE	*(almost to himself)*
	How do you think I rang the bell? , he says.
	Silence.
PJ	How long were ye in Flynn's?
SEAMIE	Long enough to eat.
PJ	Aye.
SEAMIE	And talk.
PJ	God knows, after twenty five years, ye had a fair bit of catching up to do.
SEAMIE	We had. We have.
PJ	It's a sight you can blabber now when no one wants to listen to you and you couldn't talk to your father before he died.
SEAMIE	Why should I talk to him?
PJ	He was your father.
SEAMIE	I was his son. That didn't seem to matter to him one time. I wasn't wanted. I was the cause of Mammy dying, according to him. 'Twasn't right what he did to me.
PJ	No, 'twasn't right. But you have to understand...
SEAMIE	Understand nothing. He wronged me and if I spoke to him, beyond the wan word, before he died. He'd have been forgiven. I wanted him to die unforgiven. That's

the way Clint Eastwood would have handled it. It's all over now and there's no more to be said about it.

Pause

PJ   What had ye to eat?

SEAMIE   Hah?

PJ   In Flynn's. What had ye to eat?

SEAMIE   Oh. Mary had a Neapolitan pizza and I had Chicken Wings and chips.

Pause

And two Diet Cokes.

PJ   Chips?

SEAMIE   What?

PJ   You had chips?

SEAMIE   Aye.

PJ   Had they no wedges?

SEAMIE   Oh, they had. Rakes of wedges.

PJ   But you had chips.

SEAMIE   Aye.

Pause

PJ   The wedges in Flynn's do be nice.

SEAMIE   Mighty. Far better than you'd get in Luigi's. They're home made in Flynn's.

PJ   Why didn't you have them, so?

SEAMIE   What?

PJ   If they're so nice, why didn't you have them instead of the chips?

SEAMIE   There does be garlic in the wedges.

PJ   So what?

SEAMIE   Well, I didn't want to be taking garlic or that. Just in case.

PJ   Just in case what?

SEAMIE   In case we'd be kissing or anything.

Pause

PJ   And were ye?

SEAMIE   Were we what?

PJ   Kissing.

SEAMIE   We pulled into Corky's lane.

PJ   Corky's lane?

SEAMIE	Aye.
PJ	Corky's lane?
SEAMIE	Is there a fuckin' echo in this house. I said aye.
PJ	Why didn't ye go to Mary's house when ye were that near?
SEAMIE	Mary said if you saw the light you'd be down.
PJ	She said no such thing.
SEAMIE	If you're not going to believe what I'm telling you, don't bother your arse asking me.
	Pause
PJ	Ye pulled into Corky's lane.
SEAMIE	Aye.
PJ	Then what?
SEAMIE	I kissed her.
PJ	Then what?
SEAMIE	She kissed me back.
	Pause
PJ	Did she say anything?
SEAMIE	What?
PJ	When you kissed her. Did she say anything?
SEAMIE	She said it was lovely.
PJ	Did you say anything?
SEAMIE	I said it was lovely, too.
	PJ explodes.
PJ	Now look here, gobshite. Smart ass. You got your chance and you fucked it up. There's no more Mr. Nice Guy with PJ. When the will is read tomorrow, I want you to come home here and pack whatever is yours and get the fuck out of here. If you think you're going to play me the way you played your father you have another think coming. Who do you think you are? How dare you? Going out with my woman. That's bad enough. But kissing her and whatever else.
SEAMIE	There was…
PJ	*(interrupting)*
	Shut up. I'm telling you what I want off you and if you don't do it I'll get the guards to shift you. As Edward G. said ' you're good, kid, but as long as I'm around

	you're always going to be second best and you'd better start trying to live with that.' Do you hear what I'm saying to you?
SEAMIE	Capiche.
PJ	Good. Let that be the end of that, now.
	Pause
SEAMIE	I told her.
PJ	Told her what?
SEAMIE	Told her I spoke to the old man before he died.
PJ	What?
SEAMIE	I told her I spoke to him when he told me what he had done.
PJ	What had he done?
SEAMIE	Left the place to me.
	Pause
PJ	Left what place to you?
SEAMIE	Here. This place.
PJ	He did in his hole.
SEAMIE	As the warden in Cool Hand Luke said 'what we have here is failure to communicate.' Well, I don't have to convince you. You'll find out for yourself tomorrow when the will is read.
PJ	Why would he do that?
SEAMIE	He said he did it because it was the only way he could make up for what he had done to me. It was an apology and he hoped I would see it was all he could do. That's what he told me the last time I went up to the room to him. The time Mary sent me up. That's what he told me. Then he died. So I told Mary tonight that I spoke to him. She was glad of that.
PJ	What about me?
SEAMIE	He said it wouldn't do you a bit harm to have to go out and make a living, besides mooching about here with no one for company only Meryl Streep and Julia Roberts.
PJ	Are you saying that all this is yours?
SEAMIE	It is. Unless the will says otherwise. And it doesn't.
PJ	How do you know? You never saw it.

SEAMIE	He told Mary before he told me.
	Pause
	PJ wanders around.
PJ	Well, fuck the whole lot of ye. I'll move into Mary's. At least I still have Mary.
SEAMIE	Look, sunshine, you never had Mary and you never will. Mary and myself are now what they would call in Frazier, an item. What would a woman like Mary, a Rolls Royce woman, be doing with an auld Massey Ferguson like you? Do you not think she's entitled to a man that doesn't remember where he was when Kennedy was shot.
	Pause
PJ	What am I supposed to do? What's to become of me? What will I have? Where will I go?
SEAMIE	I don't know. My Momma said 'life was like a box of chocolates, you never know what you gonna get.' You can have the videos if you like. I won't be watching them any more. I have the real thing now. And you can stay here, if you like, while we're away.
PJ	Away?
SEAMUS	We have plans. Oh, nothing finalised yet. Mary reckons she'll sell the place and we might travel a bit. She'd like to go to Italy. See her father. She says she's ready now. After tonight. Anyway, it's bedtime.
	He goes towards his father's room.
PJ	Where are you going?
SEAMIE	This will be my room now. The man of the house always slept up here. Are you coming to the solicitor?
PJ	I suppose I'll have to, to be sure. If there's any petrol after ye burning the shite out of it up Corky's lane.
SEAMIE	Didn't I tell you there's a two gallon tin in the barn? Isn't there always?
PJ	Right.
SEAMIE	See you so.
PJ	Wan Word.
SEAMIE	*(turning)*
	Seamie

PJ	Seamie. You said you told Mary you spoke to our father after he told you about the will.
SEAMIE	Aye.
PJ	Did you? Did you talk to him?
SEAMIE	I did in my hole.

He goes.

PJ goes slowly to table and sits. He stares into middle space. Suddenly he begins to cry softly.

A moment.

He scatters the jigsaw from the table with a sweep of his arm. He rises, gets videos and begins throwing them at bedroom door. During this we hear Seamie laughing in bedroom.

PJ   You bastard.

You devious bastard.

He should have killed you that time.

I should have killed you since.

Drowned you, like an unwanted kitten.

She should have brought you with her. Mammy should have.

(roaring)

I'm not going to serve another sentence.

He stops. He rushes outside. He returns with the can of petrol which he scatters on the door and all around the door area. He finds a match in his pocket. Standing in the doorway, he says, Clint Eastwood style,

There's just one question you gotta ask yourself. You feeling lucky, punk? Well, are you?

He strikes match

Hasta La Vista, baby.

He throws the match towards the petrol as light black out.

END

144

Lovely Leitrim

CHARACTERS

ROBERT CALLAGHAN   Bachelor farmer, mid sixties. Decent and hardworking.

MARTIN GALLAGHER   Leitrim farmer, early sixties, hardworking. Decent and honest with inbred work ethic.

DERMOT   London barman, late thirties.

CLOCKER LYNCH   Unemployed and good at it. Late fifties..

ANDY DONOHUE   Leitrim publican. Early sixties.

PEADAR GALLAGHER   London builder. Son of Martin and Mary Gallagher. Thirty six.

EAMONN GALLAGHER   Twenty-four. Younger son of Martin and Mary Gallagher. A reluctant farmer

MARY GALLAGHER   Early sixties. Dedicated to her husband and sons and certain in her conviction as to what is right for them.

MAUREEN   Barmaid. Twenty and naive.

MASTER   Retired school teacher. Sixty-seven. A scholar.

JACKIE LYNCH   Son of Clocker Lynch. Mid-thirties. Successful tradesman in London.

OUTLINE OF SCENES

The action of the play shifts in time and space between the private bar of the Queen's Arm's public house in London, Andy Donohue's public house in Leitrim and the kitchen of the farmhouse of Martin and Mary Gallagher in Leitrim.
Time—late 1980's.

ACT ONE

SCENE ONE

The private bar of the Queen's Arms public house in North London. It is a small, well kept bar. Polished brasses and clean furniture. The glass panel in the door bears the inscriptions *The Queen's Arms* and *Private Bar*.

Dermot, the barman, is polishing glasses.
Martin Gallagher and Robert Callaghan enter.
Martin stops to study the inscriptions.

ROBERT   Begod, Martin, a private bar. You're well got here.

MARTIN   Ah, don't mind that, Robert. I suppose it's what we'd call a snug at home.

ROBERT   Oh, I see. Right. Private.

MARTIN   You'll chance a half one?

ROBERT   Ah, sure, I suppose I might as well.

MARTIN   Two small Irish, Dermot. And two bottles of beer. In case of fire.

DERMOT   Coming up, Martin. You didn't go to the match?

MARTIN   No, we didn't bother. Ruislip is too far out. Robert here only came for the weekend and I'm showing him round the place instead. Robert was my neighbour back in Ireland. Robert Callaghan. Robert, this is Dermot. A sound Kilkenny man. If there's such a thing.

ROBERT   Ah, Kilkenny. Eddie Keher.

MARTIN   And the Hendersons.

DERMOT   And what about DJ? What do you make of England, Robert? Were you over before?

ROBERT   No. I wanted to come over once when I was younger but I couldn't get away. From what I see it's different anyway.

DERMOT	Begod, she's different surely. You'll foot no turf in Fulham, as the man says. Will you stay long?
ROBERT	I'll be going back tomorrow. I only got the chance to come over with one of the lads on the team.
DERMOT	Have you a son playing for Leitrim?
MARTIN	No, no. Robert has no son. He managed to escape marriage altogether. A neighbour of his, Young Lyons, is a sub on the team and he brought Robert over to see me.
DERMOT	That was good of him.
ROBERT	'Twas. He's good to me.
MARTIN	Oh, aye. A good neighbour.
ROBERT	*(quickly)* Are you long here yourself?
DERMOT	Too long. But I'll go back in a few years and buy my own pub. **Sound of rapping on counter in main bar.** Coming. Coming. Just rap on the counter, men, if you want me. **Dermot exits.**
ROBERT	Nice fella, that.
MARTIN	Nice fella. Sláinte.
ROBERT	Aris. **Pause** He is good to me, Martin.
MARTIN	Young Lyons?
ROBERT	Aye.
MARTIN	I know he is, Robert.
ROBERT	I wouldn't want anyone to think he was only good for his own sake.
MARTIN	Ah, sure that's your own business, Robert.
ROBERT	I suppose.
MARTIN	You'll do what's right, anyway.
ROBERT	I will.
MARTIN	Well, then, to hell with what anyone else thinks.
ROBERT	It's alright for you, Martin. When Mary died you had your two sons.
MARTIN	I had. For all the good they were to me.

ROBERT	Now, good or bad, you had them. When Stephen died, I was left on my own. Ye were gone and Young Lyons was the only one that lifted a hand to help me.
MARTIN	I know, Robert. Only just you'd wonder if his mother wouldn't be behind it. You know what they say, 'tis is her own interest the cat purrs.
ROBERT	Whether or which, how could I keep on the place without help. And he was the only one to offer. You were gone.
MARTIN	Arrah, I know, Robert. I suppose I'm only giving out to myself for not staying.
ROBERT	How could you stay?
MARTIN	No, I couldn't.
ROBERT	Well, then, shouldn't I be glad of Young Lyons. Isn't he the only one staying and trying to make a fist of it?
MARTIN	It wasn't my fault I went.
ROBERT	I'm not saying that. I'm only talking about myself being left on my own with all that work after I found Stephen in a ball in the byre.
MARTIN	There's no nature to life, Robert. It can be cruel.
ROBERT	Well, we both know that.
	Pause
	Nice pub, this.
MARTIN	Ah, grand. Grand.
ROBERT	Does Peadar come in here?
MARTIN	Oh, aye. He'll be in from the match later. We can be home with him.
ROBERT	That's a grand woman he's married to.
MARTIN	Francine? Ah, Francine is a topper. I think Peadar and herself were in the same boat when they met. Neither wanting to be where they were. And now, of course, there's the children. Grandchildren are great, Robert. They keep me going.
ROBERT	Aye, so.
	Pause
	Aye, nice place.
MARTIN	Still, it would be grand to be having this jar in Andy Donohue's instead.

ROBERT	Even with Clocker Lynch?
MARTIN	*(laughing)*
	Even with Clocker. And The Master. How are they at all?
ROBERT	The Master got old since he retired. But that hoor Clocker, God forgive me; will bury the whole lot of us.
MARTIN	He will. I heard the Master saying one night that the Americans say that the only two certainties in life are death and taxes but he had a third certainty and it was that anytime you walked into Andy Donohue's pub, Clocker Lynch would be sitting at the counter.
ROBERT	'Twas true for him.
MARTIN	And still, isn't it funny but when Peadar used to come home, Clocker was nearly the first he'd ask about.

SCENE END WITH CROSS FADE TO ANDY DONOHUE'S PUB IN IRELAND

SCENE TWO

It is mid-morning. Clocker Lynch sits at the counter, reading the racing page in a tabloid newspaper. The dregs of a pint of stout are before him. Andy Donohue has a broadsheet newspaper spread on the bar counter and is turning the pages in a disinterested manner.

CLOCKER	Begod, that's odd.
ANDY	What's that, Clocker?
CLOCKER	Jim Bolger has a yoke running in a Maiden Hurdle in Down Royal the day.
ANDY	What's strange about that?
CLOCKER	Down Royal is Dermot Weld country. Bolger usually leaves it to him. I don't see him with anything else there. He's hardly going up with one unless he's going to win.
ANDY	Maybe.
	Pause
CLOCKER	Any chance of a sub, Andy? To oil the wheels of investment, as the man says.
ANDY	How much?
CLOCKER	Gimme a pint and the change out of a tenner. If Bolger doesn't oblige, the Government will spit on Thursday, anyway.
ANDY	Alright, but don't tell anyone. I don't want the people thinking I'm a soft touch.
CLOCKER	Now, Andy, why do you think God gave me two ears and only one mouth.
	Pause
	It's quiet.
ANDY	It'll be quiet now until the holidays and some of the lads start coming home.
CLOCKER	Oh, the lads have started coming already.
ANDY	Yeah?
CLOCKER	I seen Peadar Gallagher booting it out the Drumshanbo

	road in the Volvo this morning so you can expect a visit the day.
ANDY	Oh, aye, he'll be in the day so.
CLOCKER	Pay for the conacre for the father and see what's for sale.
ANDY	I don't think Peadar has any notion of buying.
CLOCKER	You have him well smelt, Andy. Throwing shapes is all he's at. To make the father feel good. Make him think he's coming back. He has no notion. He's doing too well in England to get bogged here and I doubt if his missus will ever set foot in this place again.
ANDY	No?
CLOCKER	Took one look at us and bolted.
ANDY	Could you blame her? Wouldn't we all bolt if we could?

Pause

	Any of your bucks coming, Clocker?
CLOCKER	Not 'till Christmas, I'd say.
ANDY	They're doing alright?
CLOCKER	Better than if they stayed here, anyway. No more than Peadar Gallagher.

The door opens and Peadar Gallagher and his brother, Eamonn, enter.

Clocker immediately addresses Peadar.

	Ah, talk of the devil. You're welcome home, Peadar. I was just telling Andy I seen you this morning.
PEADAR	That's right, Clocker. Not much escapes you.
EAMONN	No big welcome for me, Clocker?
CLOCKER	Arrah fuck you, Eamonn. Amn't I kicking you out of my road every day. 'Though, mind you, I don't see as much of you since you got in tow with the Yank's daughter.
PEADAR	Will he give us a day out, Clocker?
ANDY	Oh, now, he's courting strong.
CLOCKER	She might be hooked, but she has to be reeled in yet.

They laugh.

ANDY	You're well, Peadar?
PEADAR	Keeping the good side out, Andy. Fire us up a few drinks. Gimme a brandy and a beer chaser. Eamonn?

EAMONN	No, I won't bother. I only came in with the pound for the syndicate.
	He flicks a pound coin over the bar to Andy who catches it and places it in a glass on the shelf with other coins.
	I'll go down to Gannon's for a rake of calf nuts if you give me the keys.
PEADAR	No sign of ye winning the lotto.
CLOCKER	We're confident this week. We have great numbers
PEADAR	*(giving car keys to Eamonn)*
	Here so. Keep her between the ditches. I'll meet you in Fallon's. I have to pay for the conacre. Clocker? A jar?
CLOCKER	There's two things no man should refuse, Peadar. A bishop's blessing and a free drink. I'll have the same as yourself only with a black chaser.
PEADAR	Right, Andy. How are the nags going, Clocker?
CLOCKER	Slower every day.
ANDY	He should listen to The Master.
CLOCKER	Oh, aye. The four ruinations of man.
ANDY	Fast women.
CLOCKER	Slow horses.
ANDY	Crooked cards.
PEADAR	And straight whiskey. Sláinte.
CLOCKER	Good health to the grape trampers.
	They drink.
	Pause
ANDY	Your mother is alright again, Peadar?
PEADAR	Grand, thanks, Andy. Grand.
CLOCKER	She was in Dublin?
PEADAR	Oh, aye. But they didn't have to operate or anything. She's on tablets and they say she'll be as right as rain in a month or two.
CLOCKER	Aye. So. That's good.
	Pause
PEADAR	Well, men, how are things about this place?
ANDY	Hectic, Peadar, hectic. Honest to God, only for the traffic lights, we'd never get across the road.
PEADAR	No craic, so?
CLOCKER	No craic.

ANDY	You heard about the band?
PEADAR	I did. That was a great honour.
CLOCKER	Hah?
PEADAR	Ah, now, Clocker, It's not every band that's asked to lead the New York Paddy's Day Parade. Did many go over?
ANDY	Three buses.
PEADAR	That many?
CLOCKER	Aye, but when they were coming back, Dolan only had to send one bus to pick them up.
PEADAR	Ah feck off.
CLOCKER	Honest to God. Ask Andy.
ANDY	Tell him about Jackie McGowan, Clocker.
CLOCKER	Aw, Christ, aye. Wait 'till you hear this one, Peadar.
PEADAR	Is it Tom Fadás son?
ANDY	Aye. The carpenter.
CLOCKER	When they were going through immigration beyond, Tony Quinn was ahead of McGowan and he telling the immigration officer about the band and the parade and all that. Your man asked Quinn what instrument he played and Quinn told him the kettle drum. And sez the immigration officer to McGowan and he opening his case 'I see you play the saw.' Didn't his feckin' mother put his tools on top of his clothes so as, she sez; he'd be ready for work straight away.
PEADAR	And what happened?
ANDY	He was back in Knock that night. He went on the piss in Carrick for two days and then he said he was going home to saw the two legs off his mother.
CLOCKER	*(chuckling)* I see, he sez, you play the saw.
PEADAR	Ah, the poor auld hoor. Maybe he'll get another chance.
CLOCKER	It was like being thrown out of a lifeboat back onto the Titanic.
PEADAR	Anyway, I don't think things are much better in America than they are here.
ANDY	Well, they could hardly be any worse.

PEADAR	Well, there's not much point in leaving unless you're going to something better.
	Pause
CLOCKER	Any sign of my bucks, Peadar?
PEADAR	Oh aye. I seen them on Sunday last at mass in Seven Kings. Going well.
CLOCKER	Work is slow, they tell me.
ANDY	That pace'll suit them, Clocker.
CLOCKER	Fuck off, you. Smart bollix.
	They laugh.
	Pause
	Peadar finishes his drink.
CLOCKER	Can I get you a refill, Peadar?
PEADAR	Are you carrying?
CLOCKER	Not too heavy.
PEADAR	Leave it so. I'll catch you at the weekend. I'd better go down to Fallon's and not keep this young farmer waiting. Good luck to ye.
ANDY	Good luck.
CLOCKER	See you later.
	Peadar exits.
CLOCKER	Are you carrying? Cute hoor.
ANDY	What's wrong with you?
CLOCKER	Doesn't he know shaggin' well I'm not flush of a Tuesday. Big shot. Home to pay the rent for the father and to rise dust on the roads with the big car.
ANDY	Ah, Peadar is alright, Clocker. He's not the worst of them.
CLOCKER	Peadar me arse. It's not Peadar over there, Andy. Peter. Or Pete to his friends. And did you hear the smart one about meeting my fellas at Mass?
ANDY	What about it?
CLOCKER	Christ, if I couldn't get them feckers to go to Mass here, they were hardly converted beyond in England. No, that was for your benefit, Andy. To let on he kept the faith himself.
ANDY	You're in cranky auld twist the day, Clocker.
CLOCKER	It must be my time of the month, Andy. Anyway, I'll

go down and see about this nag of Bolger's. I'll see you
this evening.

ANDY   Right, Clocker. Good luck

**SCENE ENDS WITH CROSSFADE TO QUEEN'S
ARMS WHERE MARTIN AND STEPHEN ARE
STILL IN CONVERSATION.**

SCENE THREE

ROBERT   Will you go back the year, Martin?

MARTIN   Arrah, I don't think so. What for? I'm living here now.
There's nothing there for me now only memories.
Unless for a funeral or that. And God knows, we saw
enough of them.

ROBERT   God knows.

MARTIN   It must have been very lonely after Stephen?

ROBERT   Aye. When there was only the two of us, you know.
That made it harder.

MARTIN   You know, we had some great nights, Robert.

MARTIN   The cards?

MARTIN   Aye. The cards. And the conversation. The Master.

ROBERT   He always said he felt at home on the mountain. He
could be himself. Not like below where they expected
him to be different. He had to put on an act for them.
But sure that's all gone now.

MARTIN   No card game now?

ROBERT   Who's left to play? God, Martin, the space of a few
years makes a huge difference. Hah? See down that
mountain, Martin. When I was a gossoon, I could
throw an apple into a neighbour's orchard from our
gate. Now it takes me twenty minutes on a bike to get
to Lyons.'
Hah?
All gone.
What?
Flanagans.
Gallaghers.
Mullaneys.
Quinns.
McGoverns.
All gone.
Pause

MARTIN   *(laughing)*

161

	And tell us, Robert, what would you be doing cycling to Lyons' for?
ROBERT	Nothing. I'm only saying
MARTIN	You wouldn't be courting Mrs. Lyons.
ROBERT	Stop that, Martin.
MARTIN	Arrah, I'm only joking.
ROBERT	Well don't. If Clocker Lynch heard you at that, he'd make a song out of it. God, Mrs. Lyons. I'd sooner court Jim Gilmartin's jennet.
MARTIN	As The Master would say, 'a formidable woman.'
ROBERT	A tough tulip. I often wonder, Martin, what drives that woman? What keeps her going?
MARTIN	Revenge.
ROBERT	Revenge?
MARTIN	Aye. Revenge will keep a person living far longer than love.
ROBERT	The young fella is different, Martin. More like his father. There's a bit of nature about the young fella.
MARTIN	And still. Young Lyons is sweeping up the land as they go.
ROBERT	No harm to him. Isn't it good that there's someone to take it. You were glad enough of him when you were selling your own place.
MARTIN	It wasn't my wish to sell.
ROBERT	I know. I know.
MARTIN	So?
ROBERT	Old friends shouldn't fight, Martin. Leave it at that. You'll take another half one.
MARTIN	I will so.
	Robert raps on counter.
	Dermot enters.
ROBERT	The same again, please, sir.
DERMOT	Never mind the sir. I was poor myself once, as the fella says.
MARTIN	No word of the match, Dermot?
DERMOT	Level at half time, I heard.
ROBERT	Wouldn't it be just like them to lose to London. *(proffering money)*

	Here now, take what you need out of that. I'm no good with this foreign money.
MARTIN	He'll tell you quick enough if you give him the wrong change, all the same, Dermot.
DERMOT	I'd just be thinking that. That's grand, Robert. I have enough here.
ROBERT	I suppose I'll be the cause of your next trip home so, Martin? Hah?
MARTIN	Don't be talking daft, man. Sure you're flying it.
ROBERT	Indeed'n I'm far from flying it. It has to be faced. I'm beginning to feel age, Martin. And what would I be hanging on for? I have no company. Only Young Lyons. And why should he bother with an auld fella like me? I knew it would end like this. The night Stephen and myself came back from burying your Mary, we talked about it. We knew it would end up this way. That was even before we knew you were leaving.
MARTIN	Well, I didn't know for long myself at that time.
ROBERT	I know. I'm not saying that.
MARTIN	What could I do? I couldn't have stayed, could I?
ROBERT	How do I know? You're the only one can answer that.
MARTIN	You knew the kind of Mary. She never asked much. What could I do? She knew there was no one to stay with me. What could I do?
ROBERT	I don't know.
	Dermot enters.
DERMOT	Leitrim are a point down halfway through the second half.
MARTIN	Arrah, fuck it. I'm going to loosen a button.
	He exits.
DERMOT	Ye're old friends?
ROBERT	Old friends.
DERMOT	Old friends are best, they say.
ROBERT	Does he be in much with you?
DERMOT	Martin?
ROBERT	Yes. Martin.
DERMOT	A fair bit. Mind you, not that he drinks a lot. But I think he wants the company.

ROBERT	Is he lonely like that?
DERMOT	I suppose he is. Wouldn't you be? What do you think?
ROBERT	I don't know. I was never away. Do you know I've known that man for over sixty years.
DERMOT	Long time.
ROBERT	And that's the first time I ever heard him using a four letter word.
DERMOT	How did he come to be here?
ROBERT	Did he never tell you?
DERMOT	No.
ROBERT	Well then, I can't. 'Tis his story. Let him tell it or not, as he wishes.

SCENE ENDS WITH CROSS FADE TO GALLAGHER KITCHEN

SCENE FOUR

The Gallagher kitchen. The Gallagher family are finishing dinner.

MARY Does anyone want more spuds before I bruise these few for the hens?

PEADAR Not me, anyway, Mam. I'm as full as a frog.

MARY What about you two?

MARTIN I'm alright.

EAMONN Game ball.

MARY Was there anyone in Andy's?

MARTIN Clocker, I suppose.

MARY I meant anyone apart from Clocker.

PEADAR Not at that hour of the day.

EAMONN Clocker is gas. Always enquiring about the sons and him getting a letter every week.

PEADAR Does he?

EAMONN Aye. And it doesn't be empty either.

MARTIN What are you on about. If Peadar doesn't write itself, doesn't he pay for the conacre when he comes? 'Twould take a fair few of Clocker's envelopes to pay for that.

EAMONN I'm only saying they're good to him.

MARY They're only giving back what they got.

MARTIN From who?

MARY From Clocker. Clocker was always good to his children.

MARTIN What the hell did Clocker ever give his children?

MARY He gave them his time.

MARTIN Well, God knows, he had enough of that to spare.

EAMONN Simon Carty told me one time that when the first of Clocker's went to England, he spent the first week over there looking for a job in The Irish Times.
Eamonn and Martin laugh.

PEADAR That's bullshit.

EAMONN I know. But isn't it a good one?

PEADAR	If all that amuses people here is laughing at them that went and improved themselves, it's no wonder there's so few left.
MARTIN	And tell me, Peadar, did Clocker's lads improve themselves?
PEADAR	All I know is they're not a day idle and even the English want them for paint jobs now.
MARTIN	Painters. And when they were here all they'd paint would be the road the time of an election.
PEADAR	Well, they're as dependable as there is in London now. Turn up on time, do a good job and finish on time. And no daft spending either. You might meet them in The Mother Redcap on Holloway Road of a Saturday night or in the club on Sunday but that would be the height of it.
MARY	If they had to work that hard when they were here they wouldn't have had to go at all.
PEADAR	Work hard at what? And anyway, if anyone worked that hard here, they'd be laughed at. Then when you leave they'll laugh at you if you don't kill yourself.
	Pause
	How did you fare out with the calf nuts, Eamonn?
EAMONN	I got a fiver off.
MARTIN	Good man. How did you work that?
EAMONN	I asked Gannon would he do a fiver off for cash or put the whole price in the book. When he saw the notes, he nearly took the arm off me.
PEADAR	Smart man.
MARTIN	Oh, Eamonn didn't come down in the last shower.
	Pause
PEADAR	The place is looking well.
MARTIN	Not too bad.
PEADAR	You'll have good hay.
EAMONN	We'd want to with all the bag stuff that went on it.
MARTIN	If there wasn't something there in the first place, the bag stuff wouldn't manufacture it.
PEADAR	That conacre is a waste. Why don't ye buy that place off the Quinns and be done with it?

MARY	With what shall we buy it, dear Henry, dear Henry?
PEADAR	Can't ye go in and borrow the money. I'll give ye a hand.
MARTIN	In my time and in my father's time, no bank manager's car ever pulled up on that street out there looking for money and I'm damned sure it won't start now.
EAMONN	Begod, his car is often enough on Young Lyons' street. And he's throwing money at Lyons.
MARTIN	Well, I hope Young Lyons has more than cow shite to throw at him when he comes looking for his money back.
PEADAR	And how do you expect Eamonn to bring a woman into a place this size and maybe try to raise a family in it? Hah?
MARY	There was a family raised in it before.
PEADAR	Aye. Until they were old enough to be sent away.
MARTIN	What do you mean?
PEADAR	Nothing. It's alright.
MARTIN	No, it's not alright. What are you saying?
MARY	Leave it, Martin. Leave it.
	Pause
EAMONN	It doesn't matter, anyhow. I won't be needing it.
MARTIN	Oh, begod, are you moving into Brid's place? Cute man.
EAMONN	No.
MARTIN	What then?
EAMONN	I'm not moving in anywhere. I'm moving out.
PEADAR	Where to?
EAMONN	America.
MARTIN	What? What the hell are you talking about? What the hell is he talking about?
EAMONN	I got a Donnelly Visa and I'm going to use it.
MARTIN	Donnelly visa? Donnelly visa? Do you know anything about this, Mary?
MARY	I know he got a Donnelly visa.
MARTIN	How do you know that?
MARY	Frank the Post told me when he left in the letter that that's what it was.

167

MARTIN	Why did you not mention this to me before now? How long is this craic going on? Why was I not told?
MARY	Tell what? What did I know no more than any of ye? And anyway, ye're all well fit to get things to argue about without me having to manufacture them for ye.
MARTIN	Hah?
MARY	Arrah, leave it.
MARTIN	Leave it? Leave it? He announces out of the blue that he's feckin off to America and all you can say is leave it. Well, I won't leave it. He can't go.
EAMONN	Why not?
MARTIN	That's the why. Now, forget it.
EAMONN	No, I won't forget it. Why can't I go?
MARTIN	For God's sake, man, this is your place. The land. The house. It's yours. All that was done over the years was done to have the place for you. How could you think of leaving it? It's all yours.
EAMONN	Well, I don't want it.
MARY	Eamonn, don't say that.
EAMONN	No, Mam, I don't want it. Give it to Peadar.
MARTIN	Oh, aye. And what will he do with it? Put it in the boot of the Volvo and bring it back to London? America? Christ, I never heard anything as daft in all my days.
PEADAR	What about Brid?
EAMONN	She's going with me.
PEADAR	Did she get a visa as well?
EAMONN	She doesn't need one. She was born in America. She's an American citizen.
PEADAR	When are you taking off?
EAMONN	Twelfth of next month.
MARTIN	That's what you think.
EAMONN	That's what I know. The tickets are got. Flights booked. All done. Brid's uncle has work lined up for the two of us. We'll come back here in twelve months and get married here and then go back for good.
MARTIN	Mary?
MARY	No, Martin. It's alright.
MARTIN	Eamonn, you can't go. You can't go yet.

EAMONN	Why?
MARTIN	Because...
MARY	Don't, Martin. I said don't. Don't stop him. Let him go.
PEADAR	Mother, what's wrong?
MARY	Nothing. There's nothing wrong. Can this not be talked about again? Martin, have you work to see to?
MARTIN	I have.
MARY	Well, see to it then. Eamonn, go you and see if the cattle in the low field have water.
EAMONN	But, Mam...
MARY	Go. Go, the two of you. I have a pain in my head listening to you.
	Martin and Eamonn exit.
	Pause
PEADAR	That was rough.
MARY	It was.
PEADAR	Don't worry about him.
MARY	About who?
PEADAR	Eamonn. I'll have a word with him. Straighten him out. He'll stay put. I'll handle it.
MARY	You won't.
PEADAR	What?
MARY	Don't say anything to him. Let him go.
PEADAR	What are you saying?
MARY	I'm saying to let him go. It's the only chance he has. If he doesn't go, he'll lose Brid.
PEADAR	Arrah, how could he lose Brid?
MARY	Can you not understand? She's not Irish. Oh, I know she was only twelve or thirteen when they came here but this isn't her home. She's not going to America, Peadar, as much as going home and if Eamonn doesn't go with her, he'll lose her.
PEADAR	But Mam, he can't go. You saw my father. You saw how he took it. It would kill him.
MARY	It won't.
PEADAR	Look, he spent all his life working in this place to have it for Eamonn. What is he going to do if Eamonn

	refuses it?
MARY	I'll deal with your father. He'll be alright.
PEADAR	There's something else going on here.
MARY	What do you mean?
PEADAR	There's more. There's something you're not telling us.
	You wouldn't give in like that.
MARY	Give in like what?
PEADAR	You fought for this place. Along with my father. You
	wouldn't let it go like that.
MARY	There's nothing else. What else could there be? All I
	know is what I see. What kind of a living can there
	be here for Eamonn? Always fighting rain and rushes.
	Scraping. The townies laughing at him. Let him go and
	if it breaks our hearts, it breaks our hearts.

Pause

PEADAR	There couldn't have been better luck.
MARY	Why? What do you mean?
PEADAR	It seems I needn't have gone at all.
MARY	Ah, Peadar…
PEADAR	That little bastard, Eamonn. Christ, it was the sorry
	day for me that he was born.
MARY	Peadar, what are you saying about your brother?
PEADAR	Ah, brother be damned. You don't have much soot for
	a lad twelve years younger than you when he does you
	out of your birthright.
MARY	Birthright? How? What do you mean?
PEADAR	Have you forgotten? Don't you remember why I was
	sent to England?
MARY	You went to England because…
PEADAR	I didn't went to England. I was sent to England. And
	you don't even remember. Uncle Jim there at the fire,
	one side. My father at the other and me here at the
	table trying to take in what they were saying to me.
	'There's only place for one, Peadar' my father said.
	'Go you to England and Uncle Jim will look after you
	and I'll be able to hold the place for Eamonn.' And the
	little snot sitting on the stool at my father's feet neither
	knowing nor caring what was happening.

MARY	Ah, Peadar love, stop this.
PEADAR	So, I'm shipped off to England and the problem is solved. But the problem wasn't solved, was it Mam? No. Because now, after all that, Eamonn doesn't want the place. Never wanted it.
MARY	And you did?
PEADAR	And I did. Oh God, I did. I never wanted anything else.
MARY	Peadar, how can you say that? How can you talk like that? Look how well you've done in England.
PEADAR	Oh, aye, Uncle Jim did look after me. I did well. But why? What for? What have I?
MARY	Arrah, look at you. Francine. The children. Nice house. Money.
PEADAR	Oh yeah. Money. No shortage of that if you grease the right palms and get to use shite for cement. And Francine? Poor Francine. What did we ever have in common except that we were both strangers in a foreign country? Two deportees. And my children won't even come to Ireland with me. Afraid they'll be laughed at because of their English accents. My children are ashamed of me.
MARY	Ah, Peadar, Peadar. I never knew you felt like that. You never said.
PEADAR	Said? Was there any point? Wasn't I disregarded once Eamonn arrived?
MARY	How can you think that any child can be disregarded in favour of another? You have your own children. You know that cannot be.
PEADAR	Everything seems to be my fault. Everyone wants to blame me. This will be no different.
MARY	How do you mean?
PEADAR	Wait and see. When my father comes in from the fields he'll have twisted Eamonn's leaving into my fault.
MARY	No.
PEADAR	You can bet your life on it. He'll say I unsettled him with the car and the few pound. Well, by God, I'm not carrying this one. Eamonn can forget about going. He'll play the hand that's dealt to him the same way we

	all had to.
MARY	Well, you can speak for yourself but I never begrudged playing what was dealt to me.
PEADAR	No?
MARY	No. What would make you think otherwise?
PEADAR	Ah, nothing.
MARY	What is it?
PEADAR	It was just something The Master said, one night in Andy's when he was carrying more cargo than ballast. 'Your mother,' sez he, 'is a remarkable woman. She gave up a lot.' What did he mean, Mam?
MARY	God, but you're in a bad way if you have to pay heed to anything that auld windbag might say. Do you want tea or coffee?
PEADAR	I'll take tea.
	Pause
	It's not right.
MARY	What isn't?
PEADAR	If he only knew what he was giving up.
MARY	Is it that bad away, Peadar?
PEADAR	Oh, I don't know. I suppose the worst of it is that it's away.
MARY	You could never have made the same living here, Peadar.
PEADAR	Maybe, but who said I wanted to make the same living. All I ever wanted to do was to work on the land. To stand at the road gate when the cattle were being brought in and to keep them out of the meadow. To feel the contentment of a summer's evening when the hay was saved and the turf home. To belong. To be part of something. Something that concerned me. Even only to be down in Andy's arguing with Clocker about politics. At least it would have concerned me. In England, that's none of my business.
MARY	Why?
PEADAR	Because it's not my place. I don't belong. And now, I'm beyond there. The successful man. The big shot. I spend my week negotiating contracts with fellas of all

	creeds and colours. Nice suits, nice lunches, good wine,
	occasional round of golf. Big time stuff. And then,
	Mam, do you know where I am on Sunday nights?
MARY	Where?
PEADAR	On Sunday nights, at five past eleven, I'm glued to

creeds and colours. Nice suits, nice lunches, good wine, occasional round of golf. Big time stuff. And then, Mam, do you know where I am on Sunday nights?

MARY Where?

PEADAR On Sunday nights, at five past eleven, I'm glued to Radio Eireann listening to Sean óg O'Ceallachain to hear how Aughawillan and Gortletteragh are doing. Will Drumreilly win the league? Who has the good Minor team? And every year, Mam, it takes Sean óg less time to read the results because every year, there's less teams.

MARY Ah, Peadar, don't upset yourself. That's the way life is. No one ever told us it was going to be easy.

PEADAR But does life have to be that way? Hah?

Pause

Did you ever hear of Somerset, Mam?

MARY That's a county over there, isn't it?

PEADAR Yes. Not unlike here. Leitrim with land, Jackie Lynch calls it. I was down there one day, pricing a job in Yeovil. It was a glorious day. Late June. I was driving up to Glastonbury in the afternoon to meet a surveyor and I came upon a farm where the hay was being cut. I stopped the car and got out and lay across the gate watching the machine. Then I got the smell. The smell of the new mown grass. I began to inhale it. And all of a sudden I began to cry. And I couldn't stop. I swear to God, Mam, I couldn't stop.

MARY What happened? What did you do?

PEADAR I got back into the car. Closed all the windows. Shut out the smell. I drove to Glastonbury, booked into a hotel, postponed my appointment until the next day and got very drunk. The Paddy's revenge. Hah?

Eamonn enters.

EAMONN The rooster is in the strawberry beds again, Mam.

Pause

What's up here?

MARY Nothing. I'll shift the rooster. It's time to feed the hens now, anyway. There's tea in the pot. Peadar, leave that and we'll talk about it again.

Mary exits.

EAMONN Do you want a top up?

PEADAR No. thanks.

EAMONN What was going on between the two of you?

PEADAR Ah, nothing. Nothing. So you're off?

EAMONN I'm off. What else can I do?

PEADAR You could stay.

EAMONN Why didn't you stay?

PEADAR I never got the chance.

EAMONN Did you want to stay?

PEADAR Yes. As a matter of fact, I did.

EAMONN Then you should have fought for staying.

PEADAR You think so?

EAMONN I'm bloody sure of it. When I decided to go, I knew I'd have to fight to get away and I'm going to fight. If I have to.

PEADAR Have you any idea what this is going to do to your father and mother?

EAMONN Listen, Peadar, don't try that sentimental shite on me. I know what my father thinks. I know he always thought I'd take over here. But consider my case for a second. Brid is going. The only way I can hold her is to make her marry me here. How in the name of God am I going to support anyone here? Christ, I can't even support myself.

PEADAR Things might improve.

EAMONN With twenty acres and thirty acres of conacre? Conacre that he can't even pay for himself. Are you codding me?

PEADAR It's no picnic away.

EAMONN Well, how am I ever going to know that if I don't go?

PEADAR I suppose. As long as you know what you're leaving behind.

EAMONN What am I leaving behind? God, Peadar, there has to be more to life than fighting for a few pounds off calf nuts in Gannon's.

PEADAR Ok. Well, then, will you do one thing?

EAMONN What?

PEADAR	Leave them on good terms. Talk it out with them. Explain yourself. Don't have bad blood in this house.
EAMONN	Look, if there's bad blood, it won't be my fault. I'll try to straighten things out with himself but if he wants to sulk about it, that's his problem.
PEADAR	And Mam?
EAMONN	Now, that's a conundrum.
PEADAR	What is?
EAMONN	Why is she so much in favour of me going?
PEADAR	What makes you think she is?
EAMONN	Brid and herself are as thick as thieves. Don't mind that shite about the postman telling her about the visa. Brid told her. And when Mam heard our plans she told Brid to take me away out of here as soon as she could.
PEADAR	She said that?
EAMONN	She did. She said she was afraid I'd get bogged here, like the Callaghan's, she said. Get him away quick, she said, before it's too late.
PEADAR	What's going on, Eamonn?
EAMONN	I don't know. But there's something. Anyway, whatever it is, it's making the leaving easier for us. I'm going over to Quinn's ground to dose sheep. Do you want to come?
PEADAR	No. No, I'll rest awhile and read the paper.
EAMONN	Suit yourself. I'll see you later.
	Mary enters.
MARY	Where are you off to, Eamonn?
EAMONN	Dosing sheep in the conacre.
MARY	Well, make sure you count them for that's the first question your father will ask when you get back.
EAMONN	I will.
	Eamonn exits.
MARY	God, it's gas watching them hens eating. They all have a different way. You'd swear you were in a restaurant.
	Pause
	Well, did ye talk?
PEADAR	Aye.
MARY	And?

PEADAR	I talked a bit of sense into him. Told him where his duty lay.
MARY	You did what?
PEADAR	By God, I put manners on him. The pup. Treating his father and mother like that. I told him that if he threw his birthright back at ye, I'd swing for him.
MARY	And what did he say?
PEADAR	He saw sense. He's staying.
MARY	He is not.
PEADAR	I'm telling you he is. He's going to tell Brid she'll have to marry him and stay here.
MARY	Who gave you the right to do that?
PEADAR	To do what?
MARY	To interfere in our affairs.
PEADAR	You gave me the right. When you sent me away. No one has more right to interfere than I have.
MARY	Peadar, let him go.
PEADAR	Why, Mam? Why?
MARY	Because…
PEADAR	Why? Why?
MARY	Because…Because, I'm dying.
	Pause
PEADAR	You're what?
MARY	I'm dying.
PEADAR	But you can't be. It was alright. Didn't the doctors say it was alright?
MARY	No, Peadar, they didn't. I told yourself and Eamonn that they did. But, no, they didn't tell me it was alright.
PEADAR	And what?
MARY	They said the cancer was too advanced. Inoperable is the word they use. They advised me to go home and prepare myself.
PEADAR	Mam, how could you not tell us?
MARY	I had things to see to that couldn't be seen to if you or Eamonn knew.
PEADAR	And our father?
MARY	He knows. But I made him swear on the Mass Book that he wouldn't tell.

PEADAR	And that's why you stopped him in his tracks today.
MARY	That's why.
PEADAR	Oh, Mam, I'm sorry. I am so sorry.
MARY	Don't be sorry for me, Peadar.
PEADAR	No, Mam, it's not that. I'm sorry for telling you I reared up on Eamonn. I didn't say anything to him.
MARY	Then why did you say that you did?
PEADAR	I wanted to draw you out. Find out why you were encouraging him to go. If I'd known or suspected what was wrong, I'd never have hurt you like that.
	Pause
	How long?
MARY	Left? Four months. Maybe six. Who knows?
PEADAR	Pain?
MARY	None yet. 'Twill come.
PEADAR	And my father? How is he taking it?
MARY	The poor man cannot take it in. He doesn't know what to say or do. He pretends it's not there. Like it was a sore on my face that he'd avoid looking at or referring to. On the first night I came home, when we were going to bed, he asked me if he could open the window a bit. As if it might go out or as if he thought there was going to be a smell. Since then, he just ignores it. God help him.
PEADAR	Mam, why are you so anxious for Eamonn to go?
MARY	I came out from the town to this place thirty eight years ago. I wasn't used to much at home but from the day I came here, I've had to settle for less. Your father and his parents were used to hardship but I never got used to it. But they were nice people. Good people. The kind of people that made you want to put your arms around them and love them. But when I did that, I found myself trapped. I found they left their imprint on me. Like Veronica's veil. And still, even after all these years, I still believe we deserve more. Your father is a good man. A good farmer. He has worked all the hours God made to make a farm here. This farm today is the best it will ever be. No more to come from it. And

177

what is it? Twenty acres of a battlefield where he takes on the rushes every year, never winning, never losing. Going nowhere. How can I condemn Eamonn to a life like that? I swore that I would never ask my children to settle for less.

PEADAR   So I went?

MARY   So you went, Peadar. You went because there was something for you to go to. We had no way of knowing if there was going to be anything for Eamonn, only the land, when his time came.

PEADAR   And now there is.

MARY   And now there is and he must be let go. If he doesn't he'll only live his father's life again.

PEADAR   And how will his father let him go? You saw his reaction.

MARY   Can my dying wish be refused? Can it?

PEADAR   No, he won't refuse it. If that's what it is, it will be.

MARY   Well then, that's that.

Pause

And you, Peadar, will you?

PEADAR   It has nothing to do with me anymore.

MARY   Not that. What I'm asking is will you refuse my dying wish from you?

PEADAR   What is it?

MARY   After my time, make your father sell this place and bring him to live with you in England.

PEADAR   You must be joking.

MARY   I am not. That's my wish, Peadar.

PEADAR   Mam, are you astray in the head. My father would die in England. How could you think of transporting him over there? This is his home. The land is his life. He'd smother in London. Look, Mam, I'll come over, once a month or that. Buy the conacre off the Quinns. Take a bit more interest. Hah? How does that sound?

MARY   I know you mean well, Peadar. And you would buy the conacre. And you would come over every month. For the first few months. But your home is in England now and soon you'd only be coming every second month and then maybe not in the winter at all. And then, when you'd come, you begin finding your father in Andy's with Clocker Lynch, day and night. And then you'd stop coming and to ease your conscience you'd start sending money, like Clocker's lads. And then, one morning, Young Lyons or one of the Callaghans would find him dead in the ditch at the road.

PEADAR No, Mam, no. That wouldn't happen.

MARY Are you willing to take that chance?

PEADAR Mam, don't ask me to do this.

MARY Since the day I walked in that door, I never asked anybody to do anything for me. I nursed two old people until they were dragged across the threshold of death. And during that time, I reared you as best you could be reared in a house with old people. And when I thought I had my fill done, Eamonn was born, twelve years after you. And still, I took what came and asked for nothing. See, Peadar, I had to leave home too. I have lived on this hill for thirty eight years without a single friend I could share a thought with. Even on Sunday nights, in winter, when I could maybe go to bingo or a play or something, I'd be anchored here, making the tea for The Master and the Callaghans and listening to daft talk about politics and people. And no one ever asked me was I alright or did I want anything. And you say The Master says I could have been something better. Well, I don't know if I could have been something better but I could have been something different. Now, sometime in the next few months, God will take me down from this crucifix. And I'm entitled. And I have rights. And if I never had it my way in life, then I will have it my way in death. Your father will grant me my wish. Will you, Peadar?

PEADAR Mam.

MARY Will you?

PEADAR I will. I must. But I'm telling you now that it will kill him.

MARY No, Peadar. To stay young you must stay with the

	young. His grand children will be the making of him.
PEADAR	Maybe. Maybe you're right. We'll see.
	Pause
	Christ, The Master was right. You are a remarkable
	woman.
MARY	How? In what way?
PEADAR	How can you be so cool about all this? So calm?
MARY	Sure death is natural. Won't it happen to everyone?
	Rich and poor. None of us has a freehold on life.
	Nature takes it's course. And maybe I'm more
	fortunate than a lot. At least I've had the time to see
	that everyone is left the way they should be. Because I
	know the way they should be. Whether they know it or
	not.
	Peadar moves to exit.
	Do you hear me Peadar? Whether they know it or not.
PEADAR	I hear you.
	He exits.
	Pause
	Martin enters.
	Pause
MARTIN	He knows.
MARY	Yes. He knows. Where is he gone?
MARTIN	Across the fields to the conacre. Will he be alright?
MARY	He's gone to his brother. He'll be alright. He just needs
	time to get used to it.
MARTIN	I suppose.
	Pause
	Mary, this isn't easy. This whole thing. And now
	Eamonn.
MARY	I know, Martin. But it's the right thing that Eamonn's
	doing. Don't stand in his way. Give him his chance.
	Knock on door.
MARTIN	Come in.
	Clocker enters.
CLOCKER	God save all in this house.
MARTIN	Clocker.
MARY	Clocker, you're welcome. 'Tisn't often we have the

	pleasure of your company up here.
CLOCKER	No, Mary, I'm afraid I have no head for heights. But
	I was up with the Callaghans. We have the station on
	Friday and I was getting a sup of poitin for the Canon.
MARTIN	Well, 'twon't go to loss there.
CLOCKER	No. 'Twill get a happy death.
MARY	Be sure you test it now, before you give it to the priest.
CLOCKER	Mary, I would consider that to be my moral and
	theological duty.

They laugh.

| CLOCKER | Anyway, I only called because Stephen wondered if you |

were in Andy's tonight, Martin, would you ring the AI
to call to them tomorrow. A black friesian they want.

MARY	I was just thinking that I heard a cow lowing up there
	today. You'll have a sup of something, Clocker?
CLOCKER	Indeed'n I won't, Mary. I want to get home with my
	cargo in one piece.
MARTIN	Well, you won't leave this house without taking
	something anyway. A wee shot of whiskey?
CLOCKER	Well, out of respect to the Gallaghers, then. I'll have a
	ball of malt, as long as you have one yourself.
MARY	Well, fair play to ye, but you'll look after each other,
	anyway. Sit, Clocker and I'll get the wetting.
CLOCKER	Thanks, Mary and isn't it great to see yourself looking
	so well. You're improving ahead.
MARY	A bit stronger every day, Clocker, thank God.

Mary exits.

Pause

CLOCKER	I seen you at the cattle, Martin, and I leaving
	Callaghan's.
MARTIN	Ah, just counting and keeping an eye. They're aisy
	work this time of year.
CLOCKER	Do you know what I sometimes think? I must go hard
	on a man like you to bring a beast to sell after watching
	him grow for a year and a half or maybe two years?
MARTIN	Arrah, what gradh would you leave on them. Isn't that
	what they're for?
CLOCKER	I know. But would you not get attached to them, like a

	son or a daughter, like?
MARTIN	*(as Mary enters)*
	Christ, Clocker, if they were anything like the sons I have, you wouldn't want to get too attached to them.
MARY	*(giving whiskey to men)*
	Martin, easy. Good health, Clocker.
CLOCKER	To John Jameson, deceased.
	They drink.
	Pause
	Is there something wrong?
MARTIN	Devil the hate, thank God.
CLOCKER	Is Eamonn for off?
MARY	Who told you that?
CLOCKER	No one. But I'll tell you this much, Mary. Not being a farmer makes it easier for me to tell a man that is and isn't and I know that Eamonn has as much interest in farming as I have in the foreign policy of the Bulgarian Government. And the Yankee girl never settled so he must go to hold her.
MARTIN	Jesus, Clocker, You make it sound so simple. I could strangle the hoor. I'm this last forty years working that ground. Fighting to have something to leave behind. And now he turns around and as much as tells me to stick it up my arse.
CLOCKER	Sure, who's to say he'll get on away? Who's to say he won't be back?
MARTIN	Did you ever see anyone that left this place coming back?
CLOCKER	Except in a wooden overcoat, no.
MARTIN	Well, then, that's that.
	Pause
	You were right, Clocker?
CLOCKER	How?
MARTIN	Not to give a damn about any of them. Let them off to hell and forage for themselves.
CLOCKER	Is that what you think? Hah? Is that the way it is? I never gave a shite? What?
MARTIN	That's the way it always looked.

CLOCKER	And do you think I have no nature. Am I not entitled to my own the same as anyone else? Do you think there's a day that I don't think about them? Do you not think I see the daughters in every young girl's face coming down from the rails on a Sunday? Do you think I can go to a football match without thinking about not having the lads with me?
MARY	Martin didn't mean anything by it, Clocker.
CLOCKER	I know that. It's just that you can get fed up getting taken for granted. I'm different than you, Martin. I never expected anything else. See, I knew from the first day they went to school that they were being fattened for export.
MARTIN	Christ, the whole thing seems such a waste.
MARY	You did your best, Martin. What more could you do?
MARTIN	I don't know. What the hell am I to do about Eamonn? Clocker, what would you do?
CLOCKER	Martin, the easiest job in the world is to raise another man's son. But if I was you, I'd let him go. You might as well for you'll not keep him. And if you give him your blessing, then at least he'll know he has a home where he's welcome if things don't work out for him away.
MARTIN	Easier said that done.
MARY	Anything worth doing is.
CLOCKER	Lookit. There's far too much song and dance in this place about people leaving. You'd thing no one ever left anywhere except Leitrim. Don't the English go anywhere? Hah? Why wouldn't Eamonn go? If he doesn't want to stay, what about it? That's not emigration, Martin. That's choice.
MARTIN	I suppose. It's just that a lifetime's work seems wasted.
CLOCKER	How would it be wasted? Didn't you have something to work for? If you hadn't that, what would have kept you going? If it didn't work out the way you thought it would in the end, what the hell about it? They can't take away what you did.
MARTIN	Maybe you're right. Maybe. There's more to you than meets the eye, Clocker.

MARY	Clocker was always an underestimated man.
CLOCKER	Begod, Mary, I've been called some things in my day but that's the first underestimated. I wouldn't like people to think that I was turning into a philosopher. I'd like to leave that job to The Master. Thank you both for the hospitality. You won't forget about the AI man for Stephen, Martin?
MARTIN	No, Clocker, I won't forget.
CLOCKER	Ah, sure, I could do it myself but Stephen is probably afraid I'd make a balls of it. Good luck.
	Clocker exits.
	Pause
MARY	Well?
MARTIN	Well?
MARY	Is it alright now?
MARTIN	No, Mary, it's not alright. But I'm learning these last few weeks that there's no point fighting the will of God.
MARY	Look, Martin…
MARTIN	We'll leave it at that now, Mary. We'll leave it at that. There might be more to be said about it again, but not now. We'll just leave it. Where's Eamonn?
MARY	Dosing sheep in the conacre.
MARTIN	Well, when he comes back ask him if he counted them.
MARY	I will.
MARTIN	I'll be in the castle field. Cutting tracks for the mower.
	Pause
	I anyone wants me.
	Martin exits.

SLOW FADE OUT ON MARY SITTING AT TABLE.

END ACT ONE

ACT TWO

SCENE ONE

Andy Donohue's pub on the day of Stephen Callaghan's funeral. Andy Donohue at bar. Clocker Lynch enters.

CLOCKER   Pint, Andy.

ANDY   You were in the graveyard, Clocker?

CLOCKER   I was. Christ, we seem to spend most of our time round here going to funerals. He got a good send off, anyway.

ANDY   No more than he was entitled to.

CLOCKER   I suppose.

ANDY   Isn't it hard to believe that Mary Gallagher is two years dead?

CLOCKER   I just heard Martin say last night that he'd have the anniversary mass said on Sunday before he'd go back. Time flies, as the man said when he fired the clock at the wife.

ANDY   God, that mountain is getting cleaned out altogether. Between dying and leaving, there'll soon be no one left up there.

CLOCKER   It's hard to imagine one of the Callaghans without the other one slinging out of him.

ANDY   Robert will miss Stephen.

CLOCKER   Miss him? Andy, if one of them bucks got itchy, the other fella scratched himself.

ANDY   Martin Gallagher is in good shape.

CLOCKER   Kinda lonesome, I'd say. The Callaghan's and the Gallaghers were great friends and now they've lost one a piece in the space of two years.

ANDY   Fine place up there.

CLOCKER   Fine place.

ANDY   I wonder what he'll do?

CLOCKER   Who? Robert?

ANDY	Aye.
CLOCKER	Now, that's the question. But 'tis a big place to run on your own and Robert is into pension age.
ANDY	Maybe it's time he was hanging up his boots.
CLOCKER	Well, anytime he wants to hang up his boots, he has a damsel living beside him that'd only be delighted to drive the nail in the wall for him.
ANDY	Who? Mrs. Lyons?
CLOCKER	Aye. She'd be after the place for the son.
ANDY	Arrah, away outa that, Clocker.
CLOCKER	Isn't he buying up every bit of land that comes up anywhere near him?
ANDY	Bits and pieces, maybe. But that place would run into fifty or sixty thousand. Where would he get the price of that?
CLOCKER	You never know, Andy. God is good and Uncle Sam isn't bad either.
	Maureen, a young barmaid, enters.
MAUREEN	Your dinner is on the table, Andy.
ANDY	Thanks, Maureen. Is Peggy above?
MAUREEN	No. She stayed behind to give a hand with the teas after the funeral.
ANDY	Oh, right. I'll go up so. I won't be long. If it gets busy, give me a shout and I'll come down.
	Andy exits.
CLOCKER	Well, Maureen. I'd say he can take the full hour for the grub. You'll hardly have a riot on your hands at this time of the day.
MAUREEN	No, but sure you know the way he is? Afraid I'll fill a pint wrong or not charge enough for it.
CLOCKER	No need to tell me, Maureen. I know that man since God was a gossoon. The hoor'd bottle a fart and sell it for perfume.
	The Master enters.
	Ah, there you are, Master. Can I buy you one?
MASTER	No, thank you, Clocker. To borrow a well known phrase, 'he who travels fastest, goes alone.'
CLOCKER	Shakespeare, I suppose, Master?

MASTER	Possibly, Clocker, possibly. However, I must confess to having first heard the quote used by a rather well thought of Country and Western singer who rejoiced in the name, Merle Haggard. Maureen, my love, would you be so kind as to provide a weary traveller with sustenance in the form of a small Crested Ten, to be followed to it's inevitable conclusion by a glass of your best ale.
MAUREEN	Coming up, Master. You were at the funeral?
MASTER	I was indeed.
CLOCKER	'Twas sudden, Master.
MASTER	Indeed, Clocker, sudden it was. But then death can often be sudden. As, come to think of it, can birth.
CLOCKER	I know. But he was a horrible healthy man to be getting a heart attack. I don't know was he ever a day sick in his life?
MASTER	Probably not. I've known the Callaghan brothers ever since I've been here and I cannot recall ever hearing either of them complain of ill-health.
MAUREEN	Did you teach him, Master?
CLOCKER	*(laughing)* Ah, jay, that's a good one.
MAUREEN	What's wrong?
MASTER	Enlighten me, my dear. How long is it since we first had the pleasure of beholding your comely countenance?
MAUREEN	What?
CLOCKER	How long are you working here?
MAUREEN	Oh. About four months.
MASTER	Indeed. In that case you could not be reasonably expected to be acquainted with the age profiles of the proletariat. For the record, the deceased was sixty three years of age. I, on the other hand, retired two years ago, having stumbled to the age of sixty five, at which point, the Department of Education, lest persons of my vintage continue to inflict scholarship upon the masses, changed the locks on the school doors. Ergo, on the basis that the deceased commenced his primary education at the age of four, for me to have

had the privilege of dispensing knowledge to Stephen Callaghan, I would have had to embark upon my teaching career at the age of eight. I know of only two people who achieved that distinction. One was a carpenter's son who developed a penchant for teaching in temples and the other was a musician named Wolfgang Amadeus Mozart.

CLOCKER He's saying he didn't teach him, Maureen.

MASTER No, Maureen. But I did better than that. I knew him. And I toast his memory.

CLOCKER Slainte and Amen to that.

MAUREEN I can't place him at all.

CLOCKER Ah, you can, Maureen. Did you never see the tractor on a Saturday with Stephen, Lord have mercy on him, driving and Robert sitting in the transport box with the bag of groceries.

MAUREEN Is it Barnie and Beanie?

CLOCKER Who?

MAUREEN That's what the boss calls them.

CLOCKER Well, them's your men.

MAUREEN Which of them is dead?

CLOCKER The pilot. Stephen. Robert is grounded. Not that he was ever too far off the ground in a transport box.

MAUREEN I don't think I ever saw them in here.

CLOCKER *(laughing)*
I wouldn't think so. No.

MASTER I trust, Clocker, you are not attempting to attach a designation of parsimony to the brothers Callaghan?

CLOCKER What?

MASTER You're not saying they were mean?

CLOCKER Ah, no, Master. No, now, fair play. But I mean they wouldn't give themselves much time for drinking.

MASTER Agreed. But on the all too rare occasions when they chose to imbibe in any of our local hostelries, neither were ever found wanting in the decency stakes.

CLOCKER True for you, Master, true for you. Still, they have a bit of a name for gathering money.

MASTER Have they? I wonder how they acquired that?

CLOCKER	Ah, sure you know the way people talk.
MASTER	Yes. I might claim to have passing acquaintance with the methods of begrudgery.
CLOCKER	Sure some of the stories about that pair are priceless.
MAUREEN	Like what, Clocker? Tell us one.
CLOCKER	Arrah, now, there's one of them dead and it's not right to be talking.
MASTER	My dear Clocker, of all the admonitions issued to the Irish, the exhortation to speak well of the dead is unquestionably the most hypocritical and least likely to be observed since the dead offer us such an inviting target. If, therefore, you are privy to some tit-bit which will enrich our dear Maureen's life, do not, in any way, feel constrained from sharing it by the fact that the subject of the canard has passed away.
MAUREEN	That's right, Master. We'll be dead long enough. What is it, Clocker?
CLOCKER	Well, Willie Higgins. You know Willie, Master? From Ballyoran?
MASTER	Ah, yes. Liam O'Higin. I remember.
CLOCKER	Well, Willie was doing an extra postman last Christmas and he was up at Callaghan's one morning and when he went into the house there was the pair of them, sitting at the kitchen table, eating out of the one egg.
MAUREEN	*(laughing)*
	God, that's famous.
CLOCKER	Hard men.
MASTER	They were hard on no one only themselves.
	Pause
CLOCKER	Maureen, put on another pint for me. I must inspect the facilities. Isn't that the way to say it, Master?
MAUREEN	Ok, Clocker.
	Clocker exits.
	He's great craic, Master, isn't he?
MASTER	I beg your pardon?
MAUREEN	Clocker. Great sport. You know. A good auld laugh.
MASTER	I could, if required, festoon the inestimable Clocker

	Lynch with adjectives without ever having recourse to any of the ones you have just selected for him.
MAUREEN	How do you mean?
MASTER	Oh, never mind, my dear. The man with the befitting nickname is, as you say, great craic.
MAUREEN	Oh, yeah, he was telling me how he got the name.
MASTER	He was what?
MAUREEN	Yeah. How they call him Clocker on account of all the forwards he knocked out when he was playing football.
MASTER	Is that what he said?
MAUREEN	Why? Is it not true?
MASTER	Would Clocker tell a lie, I ask you? And verily, there is many a true word spoken in jest. Mind you, I have always felt that, with nine children to their name, the sobriquet Clocker would have been more accurately attached to his wife.
MAUREEN	Whatever you say, Master. Will I get you a refill?
MASTER	No, Maureen, thank you. Our revels are now ended and the dining room, chez nous, will be opening about now. Parting is such sweet sorrow.
MAUREEN	Is that another one of Merle Haggard's?
MASTER	*(laughing)*
	No. At least not yet.
	Master exits.
	Pause
	Clocker enters.
CLOCKER	Is the professor gone?
MAUREEN	Gone for grub. One pint of best, Clocker, with the shamrock on top.
CLOCKER	Thanks, Maureen. God, that fella is a ferocious gob-shite.
MAUREEN	Who? The Master?
CLOCKER	Ah, Master me arse. Going around talking with a plum in his mouth and using jawbreakers in case anyone would think he was one of us.
MAUREEN	Ah, I think he's nice.
CLOCKER	Above in that school like Lord Muck, quoting Latin and shaggin' Shakespeare to young fellas that should

	have been learning how to mix cement and roof houses.
MAUREEN	But sure he wouldn't have been able to teach them that.
CLOCKER	Well, then, couldn't he have stopped shouting at them
	about saints and scholars.
MAUREEN	Arrah, now, Clocker, you have to have a bit of learning
	or you'll get nothing.
CLOCKER	Tell us, Maureen, were you at Mass on Sunday?
MAUREEN	Of course I was.
CLOCKER	And tell us, how many professors and fellas with
	degrees did you see there?
MAUREEN	What would the likes of them be doing round here?
CLOCKER	Now you have it. What would the likes of them be

doing round here. It makes no odds how much or
how little learning you get, there's nothing round
here for you anyway. And I'll tell you, you'll hear no
Shakespeare from McAlpine or John Laing. Nothing
here. Fellas like Stephen that was planted this morning
and his brother working their arses off on the side of a
hill, trying to make money out of rushes. Above on a
bloody mountain where they have to take the horns off
the cattle so they can get their heads between the rocks
for a bit of grass. Now, they're disappearing. too. All
that'll be left soon in this place will be fellas like myself
and the Master. One half too lazy to work, one half too
brainy.

Arrah, what's the point in talking .

(moving towards exit)

Throw the light on the dartboard, Maureen. Quigley
will be in soon and I might take a quid off him in a
Shanghai.

Cross fade to Queen's Arms.

SCENE TWO

As scene opens Martin and Robert are entering. They have been for a walk.

MARTIN Well, what do you think?

ROBERT I didn't think I'd see that many trees. You wouldn't see trees like that on a street in a town in Ireland.

MARTIN The English are great for the trees. But Francine reckons the French are even fonder of them.

ROBERT And there's a lot of green too, isn't there?

MARTIN Not as much as at home, though.

ROBERT Ah, now, I'd never stick the noise, but.

MARTIN You'd get used to it. I thought it was wicked when I came first but I'd hardly notice it now.

ROBERT You'll hear no corncrakes anyway.

MARTIN No, begod. But sure you'd hardly ever hear them at home now, either.

ROBERT You miss the land?

MARTIN Not too bad now. When I came over first, I did, but Peadar got me an allotment and I like that.

ROBERT An allotment?

MARTIN Aye, it's a plot of rented ground. I grow vegetables there. I spend a lot of time there. I like it.

ROBERT Rented ground?

MARTIN Aye. It's leased from the council.

ROBERT So you're still at the conacre.
        They laugh.

MARTIN Ah, sure the poor Paddy will always have to rent. Never have the price of anything. Will we have another bottle of beer while we're waiting for Peadar?

ROBERT Alright, but I don't want to take too much or I'll be running to the lavatory all night.
        Martin raps on the counter and Dermot enters.

MARTIN Two light ales, Dermot.

DERMOT Ye had a stroll?

MARTIN	Ah, just round the block, as the Yanks say. And down to the park.
DERMOT	You'll stay, Robert?
ROBERT	Indeed'n I will not.
MARTIN	I wonder did they win?
DERMOT	Oh, they got through alright. Sorry, I thought ye knew.
ROBERT	Ah, well, that's good news.
DERMOT	Aye. Close enough. Three points.
MARTIN	Jaysus, that was tight.
ROBERT	Young Lyons hardly got a game if it was that close.
DERMOT	Who will they be playing next?
MARTIN	Mayo. God help us.
DERMOT	How will they do?
ROBERT	They'll have a job keeping the ball kicked out to Mayo. **Dermot exits.**
MARTIN	The Lynches might be back from the match with Peadar.
ROBERT	Aye?
MARTIN	Aye. They come out here the odd Sunday.
ROBERT	They're doing well?
MARTIN	Cleaning up. Seamie is only back from America.
ROBERT	America. Clocker's son. Hah? Peadar is going well?
MARTIN	Ok, I suppose. Not as good as he was. He says there's far too many blacks and Pakistanis willing to work cheap. And he lost a fair bit on a job in Somerset. What the hell he was doing with work in Somerset is beyond me.
ROBERT	Where's Somerset?
MARTIN	Away over the other side of England. Lying up against Wales. He's done a lot of work over there. Jackie Lynch says it's because it reminds him of Leitrim. Well if it does, he made no more money in it than he would have in Leitrim. You know, Robert, Peadar changed. He changed a lot.
ROBERT	How do you mean, Martin?
MARTIN	Since his mother died. And since I sold the place. His nature changed. He seems to be away a lot. I think he's drinking more than he should. And drink isn't agreeing

	with him any more. You know, there's things. Ah, but sure it's not my place to say anything.
ROBERT	Well, you're his father.
MARTIN	Arrah, he's a grown man, Robert. He has his own family. If it was Eamonn, 'twould be different. I'd be used to shouting at him.
ROBERT	Do you hear from Eamonn?
MARTIN	He rings every fortnight. And he sends a few dollars for porter every month. Now, that's the boy that's doing well.
ROBERT	That was the strangest turn out I ever saw.
MARTIN	'Twas peculiar surely. And me to try everything I knew to keep him at home and I blamed the Brid girl for bringing him away and who would ever think that she wouldn't settle beyond and would have to come back?
ROBERT	And Eamonn settled in alike a native.
MARTIN	Never looked back.
ROBERT	I never thought that pair would break up.
MARTIN	Well, wasn't it better they did then than have it happening later. How is Brid getting on at home?
ROBERT	Oh, grand. Grand. Working in Carrick.
MARTIN	A grand girl.
ROBERT	You heard the news?
MARTIN	News?
ROBERT	About Brid? Who she's going out with now?
MARTIN	No. Who?
ROBERT	Young Lyons.
MARTIN	Get away outa that.
ROBERT	God knows. This few months.
MARTIN	Well, good luck to the pair of them. She'll be a fair damsel if she passes the Mammy's inspection.
ROBERT	Oh, I think she got her feet under the table already. I'd say it'll be a wedding.
MARTIN	Well, it'll be a change from a funeral.
	Pause
	Look, Robert, if Peadar has drink on him when he comes, we'll leave.
ROBERT	Aye?

194

MARTIN	It's just that he can be a bit thick. Loud. You know.
ROBERT	I'd never have thought that of Peadar.
MARTIN	Well, things change. But we'll leave. Alright?
ROBERT	Alright. Whatever you think best.
	Jackie Lynch burst into room.
JACKIE	Up Leitrim.
	Dermot enters.
DERMOT	Well, Jackie.
ROBERT	That's a son of Clocker Lynch's, anyway.
JACKIE	Robert Callaghan. You're welcome to the city of London. How do you like it? Are you staying long? You didn't go to the match?
MARTIN	You wouldn't know which question to answer first, Robert.
JACKIE	Doesn't matter a shite. What can I get ye? Answer that one first.
MARTIN	Any sign of Peadar?
JACKIE	He'll be back later. He met two of the lads from Aughavas and he went into the clubhouse with them. *(aside to Dermot)* She's halfway to Paradise already.
DERMOT	Oh, Christ. Not again.
JACKIE	Well, men, what'll be?
MARTIN	I don't think we'll bother, Jackie. We told Francine we'd be back for tea.
JACKIE	Oh, begod, keep in with the Frenchwoman, anyway. It's hard to beat the rake of parlez-vous. Throw us up a lager, Dermot, before Peadar arrives and starts the shorts. Robert, we were awful sorry we couldn't get back for Stephen's funeral. We were awful sorry to hear about it.
ROBERT	I know that, Jackie.
JACKIE	Seamie was in the States at the time and I couldn't get away.
ROBERT	Your father sends his regards.
JACKIE	He's well.
ROBERT	Bully. The brother isn't with you?
JACKIE	Seamie's gone to Highgate to price a house job.

ROBERT	On Sunday?
MARTIN	Days of the week don't count here, Robert.
JACKIE	Especially when the work is scarce. Well, good luck to all hands.
ROBERT	Good luck.
MARTIN	Cheers.
ROBERT	Are you for home the year, Jackie?
JACKIE	Oh, aye. Third weekend in September. To see Leitrim in the All Ireland Final.
DERMOT	Playing what? Pocket billiards?
JACKIE	Fuck you. They have a better chance of being there than Kilkenny.
DERMOT	Ah, Jackie, we don't wait that long. We usually have our trip over on the first Sunday in September.
MARTIN	Don't mind this pair, Robert. You mightn't think it but they're the best of friends behind all that.
JACKIE	We will be back, Robert. Aren't we every year. Could be a big wedding the year, Martin, I hear? Hah?
MARTIN	Aye. So. So I hear.
JACKIE	Funny one that. The way it worked out.
MARTIN	Aye
ROBERT	No sign of a wedding on yourself, Jackie?
DERMOT	What would he be buying a cow for and him able to get the milk for nothing?
ROBERT	Is that the way it is?
JACKIE	Don't heed that bollocks, Robert. I'm courting strong. **Pause** This week.
ROBERT	And Seamie?
JACKIE	That fella is too busy to get married.
MARTIN	He'll marry yet.
JACKIE	Well, it'll have to be to a pregnant woman for he wouldn't take the time to do it.
ROBERT	What was he doing in America?
JACKIE	Fuck all. Just went over for a look.
MARTIN	Six months is a fairly long look.
JACKIE	Arrah, what would you see in a fortnight?
ROBERT	Were you ever over yourself?

JACKIE	Two years ago. But we're finishing a big job and as soon as that's done, I'm off again.
MARTIN	America?
JACKIE	Naw. I think I'll head for Australia. New Zealand. Down that direction.
ROBERT	For long?
JACKIE	I don't know. Five, six, seven months. As long as it takes. Seamie is back so it's my turn now.
ROBERT	Begod, Clocker would be proud of ye.
JACKIE	I hope they are. How are they keeping? Plenty of football and ceilidhs?
ROBERT	Oh, aye. Enjoying themselves.
MARTIN	And why wouldn't they? Didn't Clocker work long enough?
JACKIE	Now, Martin, as you know, doing nothing can be hard work, too. Anything my father had, he held onto, anyway.
ROBERT	This is no place for chat like that.
JACKIE	I'm only just saying
MARTIN	I was only codding, Jackie.
JACKIE	Fair enough. But we never thought there was anything funny about Clocker. He was always good to us. Minded us well. We never ate too much but we always ate enough and we never went anywhere with the arse out of our trousers.
ROBERT	Did you ever think of going home? For good, like?
JACKIE	Home? Where's home, Robert? Sure, as the man says, wherever I hang my hat. What's back there? I didn't ask to be born there so what attachment have I to it? We can go to see the auld pair whenever I want and sure we're on the phone twice a week.
MARTIN	And the letters.
	Pause
JACKIE	And the letters. So we owe Leitrim nothing. We'll leave it to the archaeologists.
	Peadar enters. While not drunk, he has been drinking and his demeanour reflects that fact.
PEADAR	*(shouts)*

	Up Leitrim.
JACKIE	Up Leitrim.
PEADAR	Usual, Dermot. And a beer chaser. Dad? Robert?
MARTIN	No, thanks, Peadar. We're just going.
PEADAR	Arrah, Jaysus, have one. 'Twon't kill ye.
MARTIN	We had three already. We told Francine we'd be back for the tea.
PEADAR	Tell her to leave me out of the pot. I want to talk to Jackie about a job. I'll get a Chinese later.
MARTIN	She's hardly expecting you anyway. Mind yourself. Are you right, Robert?
ROBERT	Right, Martin. Goodbye, Jackie. I'm glad to have met you. I'll tell your father you're fine. Goodbye to the Kilkenny man, too. Whenever you're over, come up to Carrick. You'll be welcome.
DERMOT	Now, Robert, do you not think I see enough Leitrim men all year without spending my holidays with them as well.
ROBERT	I'll see you later, Peadar.
PEADAR	Could happen, Robert. Good luck, men.
	Martin and Robert exit.
PEADAR	Jackie?
JACKIE	What?
PEADAR	A scoop?
JACKIE	A lager.
PEADAR	Arrah, take a fuckin' short. That stuff is only for washing hearses.
JACKIE	No, it'll do me. We have an early start and a hoor of a high job tomorrow.
PEADAR	Take one yourself, Dermot.
DERMOT	Cheers, Peadar. I'll take a light ale. In honour of the victory.
PEADAR	Some victory.
JACKIE	Did you ever see such shite?
PEADAR	Never.
JACKIE	Jaysus, if London trained at all, they'd have beaten them.
PEADAR	Do you know what? If all the Leitrim lads in London

	got together, they'd put out a team that'd beat them.
JACKIE	Sure there's feck all left in Leitrim to play football now. They're all in England and America, singing back at it. *(singing)* 'Last night I had a pleasant dream'
PEADAR	It's a good while since anyone from Leitrim had a pleasant dream.
	Pause
JACKIE	Young Lyons didn't get a run.
PEADAR	Ah, Jaysus, Jackie, they're bad but they're not desperate.
JACKIE	You didn't wait for him?
PEADAR	The coach is passing here, so Dolan will drop him off. There was a team meeting after.
JACKIE	Emergency session, I'd say. I suppose he'll land soon.
PEADAR	Aye. Dripping sincerity. 'Thanks very much, Mrs. Gallagher. It's very good of you to have us, Mrs. Gallagher'
JACKIE	Mrs. Gallagher?
PEADAR	Francine. Jaysus, she didn't know who he was talking to.
JACKIE	Oh, a mannerly boy. Well brought up.
PEADAR	That yoke is only a fuckin' suck. Hit me again, Dermot. No chaser.
JACKIE	Have you a job?
PEADAR	What?
JACKIE	A job. You were saying to your father that you wanted to talk to me about a job.
PEADAR	Arrah, shite. Where would I get a job?
JACKIE	Have you nothing on?
PEADAR	Roofing in Yeovil.
JACKIE	You'll get found out with that bird yet.
PEADAR	Who'll find out? Unless they're told.
JACKIE	No one will be told. But you'll get careless. You're spending too much time in Somerset.
PEADAR	Isn't there work in it? Amn't I living out of it?
JACKIE	Only as long as you're shacked up with yer wan. That finishes, you're finished.

PEADAR	What are you saying?
JACKIE	Bi Churamach. You have a lot to lose.
PEADAR	I lost anything I had to lose when I came over to this kip. We all do.
DERMOT	Ah, now, you gained a fair bit too. So did you, Lynch.
JACKIE	Me? Hah? I'm still hanging round with fellas that are drinking more than they're eating.
PEADAR	Why don't you go back home, so?
JACKIE	Me?
PEADAR	Aye.
JACKIE	No fuckin' way. I burnt the bed the day I left that place. Anyway, sure we're all scattered now. Clocker reckons that when he dies, it'll be cheaper to send him to England or America to plant him than to have us all coming home.
DERMOT	Would you not like to go home?
JACKIE	For what?
DERMOT	Maybe start something. Or buy a place.
PEADAR	Oh, aye. I had a great idea for a factory in Leitrim but I couldn't get the money to back me.
DERMOT	What was it? What were you going making?
PEADAR	I was going making For Sale signs for auctioneers. Huge demand in Leitrim. **Peadar and Jackie laugh.** No, Dermot, you see Lynch and myself, despite the generations of armed and unarmed struggle against Her Majesty's Imperialist Forces, find ourselves, on this pleasant June evening, in our real spiritual shelter, where we demand and receive sanctuary from the realities of life—nestling in The Queen's Arms. **Young Lyons enters. He carries a kit bag. Peadar immediately addresses him.** But, Jaysus, here comes our saviour. Our trump card. Dermot, this is our ace in the hole. Our secret weapon. Young Lyons.
LYONS	Hello, men. I found ye alright.
DERMOT	Hello
PEADAR	Picture the scene, Dermot. Location, McHale Park,

Castlebar. Occasion, Connacht Football Championship
Final. Time, ten minutes to play. Position, Mayo
leading by nineteen points. Situation, hopeless.
(sings)
'But hark a voice like thunder spake'
Strip off, Lyons. Enter our number sixteen. Our super
sub. Leitrim's Roy of the Rovers. Ten minutes later,
final whistle. Result?

JACKIE Mayo win by thirty one points.

PEADAR Ah, feck, Jackie, you heard it before.

LYONS Well, Jackie, how is things?

JACKIE If they were any better I'd don't think I'd stick it. Are you having a drink or are you in training?

LYONS Ah, sure, I don't drink at all anyway. I'll take a bottle of orange.

PEADAR Are you still a pioneer?

LYONS Aye. Still with them.

JACKIE The piners. Put them up, Dermot.

PEADAR Andy named out the Pioneers to Clocker one night and when he was finished, Clocker said that they might as well be Pioneers because no one would drink with them anyway.

JACKIE This is Dermot. Kilkenny man.

LYONS Oh, the Fennellys.

PEADAR Christy Heffernan.

LYONS Jim Treacy.

PEADAR Who?

DERMOT Now, there's a Leitrim man that knows hurling.

LYONS Slainte.

JACKIE Bottoms up, old chap.

Pause

LYONS We weren't great the day.

JACKIE No perjury committed with that statement.

LYONS We'll hardly work Mayo?

PEADAR Work Mayo? Work Mayo? The only hope ye have of beating Mayo is that the entire football population of Mayo, down to under fourteens, gets infected with Aids.

	Pause
JACKIE	In the next two weeks.
PEADAR	In the next two weeks.
JACKIE	Unlikely.
DERMOT	These fellas are very encouraging.
LYONS	Well, 'twas always easier to throw stones than to carry them.
PEADAR	What?
LYONS	Nothing. Nothing.
PEADAR	No. No. What do you mean?
LYONS	Well, you'd get fed up sometimes. If you just try to improve things. Improve anything. The vultures are waiting. To pick any bit of flesh off anything. To belittle. Alright, we mightn't work Mayo the year but we worked them before and we would never have done that if we didn't keep trying. Criticise away at us for not beating them but don't belittle us for trying. Because if we stop trying are we ever going to see the light of day again?
	Pause
JACKIE	*(to Peadar)*
	What the fuck is he talking about?
PEADAR	No, wait, Jackie. Listen. Listen up. This is the voice of the New Ireland we keep hearing about. The educated classes.
LYONS	I got no more education than the rest of you.
PEADAR	Oh, but you did. Weren't you one of The Chosen People? Didn't I often hear the Master, in Donohue's, describe you as one of his acolytes. Didn't he, Jackie?
JACKIE	One of his what?
PEADAR	Acolytes.
JACKIE	Did he? Well, I'm glad he never called me that, whatever it is. My father would have killed me.
PEADAR	'That Young Lyons has brains. A scarce commodity. If he uses them, he need never be a farmer.'
JACKIE	Jaysus, The Master was gas, too. About a century behind the times. Still, isn't if funny how stuff stuck with you from school. I know the first line of about

	two hundred poems. And as for songs. I mind one great June day, he brought us all out the field behind the school to hear a rake of larks and then we had to learn The Lark in the Clear Air. And, bejaysus, I still find myself singing it at work
PEADAR	A lark would have some job finding clear air to sing in around here.
DERMOT	How are things beyond?
LYONS	Same as ever. Less of us left every year.
DERMOT	You never thought of leaving yourself?
LYONS	Oh, indeed I did. Often. But home is home and I suppose I always thought it was worth fighting to stay in it. Are you long here yourself?
DERMOT	Too long. But I'll go back in a few years and buy my own pub.
LYONS	In Kilkenny?
DERMOT	Probably.
LYONS	Good country.
JACKIE	*(to Peadar)*
	That record of Dermot's is getting a bit scratched.
PEADAR	It's like listening to The Fields of Athenry.
DERMOT	What's that?
PEADAR	Ah, nothing. I'm just thinking if you're going to buy that place you'd want to stop giving the price of it to Ladbroke and Joe Coral.
LYONS	Do you like a flutter, Dermot?
DERMOT	Arrah, an odd auld touch.
JACKIE	An odd one? Jaysus, Dermot, if you were in Coventry when Lady Godiva was going through, you have been looking to see how the horse was acting on the ground.
PEADAR	Are you stuck to the ground or something?
LYONS	What?
PEADAR	It's time you made a counter attack.
LYONS	What?
JACKIE	It's your round. Up again, Dermot.
PEADAR	So, tell me, why didn't you take the Master's advice and use your brains? Why did you get stuck with the farming?

LYONS	Because that's what I wanted to do.
DERMOT	That sounds fair enough to me.
PEADAR	Oh aye? And so it is, Dermot, so it is. If it was left at that. But no, Young Lyons here was not content to be just a farmer. He wanted to be the biggest farmer. So now we have our own version of The Virginian riding the plains of Leitrim.
JACKIE	Hoss Cartwright at The Ponderosa.
LYONS	What's wrong with that? I paid well for anything I have and I have to work every hour God sends to hold on to it. What's wrong with that? If no one else wants it? If no one else wants to stay and look after it, why are you so bitter against anyone that does?
PEADAR	Maybe we didn't all get the option.
LYONS	We all got the chance and anyone that isn't the way they want to be has only themselves to blame.
PEADAR	Versatile man, this, Dermot. Farmer, footballer and now, philosopher. What next, I wonder? Politics?
JACKIE	The me-fein party.
PEADAR	By Christ, if you go into politics, I'll assassinate you.
LYONS	Well, no more than anything else, someone has to do that, too.
PEADAR	Hah?
LYONS	To care about things. To do something.
JACKIE	To wear the number sixteen jersey.
LYONS	Exactly.
PEADAR	'They also serve who only stand and wait.'
JACKIE	Milton. On His Blindness.
PEADAR	Maith an Fear, Mac an Uaradoir.
JACKIE	Mac an Cloig. Uaradoir is a watch.
DERMOT	God, how do you remember that?
JACKIE	When you're called a thing often enough, you remember it.
LYONS	I might be old fashioned but I think it's an honour to wear the Leitrim jersey. Even if it's only as a sub.
PEADAR	That's all you'll ever be. A fuckin' sub.
LYONS	We'll see.
PEADAR	I hear you're playing sub for our Eamonn now, as well.

JACKIE	*(clutching his groin)* Ow.
LYONS	It's not my fault if your Eamonn couldn't hold on to Brid.
PEADAR	That's another way of saying if no one else wants the land, you'll have it. Is that the way with Brid? Hah? Another scalp? Eamonn doesn't want her, so you'll buy? Hah?
LYONS	Fuck off.
PEADAR	Language. Language.
JACKIE	I don't remember the Master teaching us that one. That must have been reserved for the acolytes.
PEADAR	No, Jackie, but all us rats react the same way when we're cornered.
LYONS	You think your shite is marmalade, Gallagher. Arriving back in Ireland with your big car and the cigar hanging out of your mouth. Blowing about the French wife and all the work you have on. But all you are is a thick Paddy that the English get to do work that they wouldn't do themselves. But you'll do it. And be glad of it. But you wouldn't do it at home half as quick. You wouldn't be seen doing it. Oh, no. No. What did you ever do for Ireland?
PEADAR	Do for Ireland?
LYONS	Aye. Do for Ireland.
PEADAR	Jesus Christ. Is it not enough that I have to be here? In this kip of a country. To feed myself. To rear children. To mind them. To give a start to every hoor's son that lands on my doorstep. Is that not enough? Have I to do something for Ireland, as well? Have I to free Ireland?
JACKIE	Sean South from Garryowen.
LYONS	Well, Sean South isn't forgotten, is he?
PEADAR	Jaysus, Dermot, add Freedom Fighter to that list I gave you there. Free Ireland, my arse.
LYONS	What do you think of that, Jackie?
JACKIE	What does it matter? Sure it's only an auld place, the same as any other. A place to leave. To come from.
LYONS	You don't care, either.

PEADAR	Clocker's buck. What would he care about? Jaysus, Dermot, isn't that some affliction to carry through life?
DERMOT	What?
PEADAR	Being known as Clocker's son.
JACKIE	It never bothered us.
PEADAR	No?
JACKIE	No. Why should it? It never bothered him.
PEADAR	Then why did he not tell the barmaid in Donohue's the truth? Why did he tell her he got the nickname for clocking forwards when he was playing football?
JACKIE	Who told you he said that?
PEADAR	The Master. Now, that doesn't sound like a man that wasn't bothered.
LYONS	Arrah, leave it, can you not? It's that long now since Clocker stole them watches that maybe he's entitled to think it's forgotten.
JACKIE	But it's not. And neither will it be as long as there's fuckers like Gallagher that'll use anything to keep men in their place. But we don't mind. Because we won't stay in our place for him. Pass no heed of that bollocks, young fella.
PEADAR	No, don't. But don't pass much heed of Lynch, either.
LYONS	Why not?
PEADAR	Because Clocker's crowd never gave a shite about anything or anyone.
JACKIE	No? Well, we minded ourselves. And we minded our own business.
PEADAR	Oh, surely. The family that had the two parties.
LYONS	What two parties?
PEADAR	Did you never hear that? The Lynch family celebrated the Mammy and Daddy's Silver Wedding on the same day as Jackie's twenty sixth birthday.
JACKIE	And do you know why? Because the Lynches never pretended to be anything they weren't. Clocker was always Clocker. Never anything else. You know where you stand with the Lynches. I told Clocker. The time of the party. I told him. They'll laugh at it, I said. They'll jibe about my age. And Clocker said 'feck them, let

them laugh.' Are we going to let them stop us from having a good night? We are what we are.' And we had a good night. And they jibed. And even Gallagher there, that should know better, jibes. But let him. The next job we do for him, I'll add a monkey for that jibe. Because no one lives rent free in my head. Some people think I should spend my life apologising for being born, for being Clocker's son. But we can't all be the sons of Bishops.

PEADAR Stop, Jackie. I didn't mean anything. I was only acting the bollocks.

JACKIE No, Peadar, fuck you. I'll have my say. We don't all have to bow and scrape to the mighty Gallagher. We were laughed at all our lives. And Clocker told us we'd never be anything at home, only Clocker's sons, so we'd better go. So we went. And we didn't get much education so we had to fall back on our brains. But every cripple finds his own way of walking and we managed. So, Peadar, my friend, I'll carry my own cross but I won't carry yours. This bollocks, Lyons, is right. You might be better off doing what you want to the odd time instead of always doing what you think people expect of you.

PEADAR Well, Young Lyons, what do you think of all that? Wasn't that some spake from a son of Clocker's?

LYONS It's what he believes, anyway.

PEADAR Oh, is that the official response from Lord Leitrim?

DERMOT Cool it, Peadar. Cool it.

PEADAR Ah, but Dermot, auld stock. You need to know what you're dealing with here. This is Lord Leitrim, our benevolent landlord. And when Lord Leitrim talks, as he did earlier, about vultures, he conveniently forgets that he's sitting on the top branch himself. That shite there bought every bit of land that came up around him according as the people died or left. But when Stephen Callaghan died, he couldn't persuade Robert to sell and he had to change tack. He has now adopted a policy of peaceful infiltration. No like your usual freedom fighter at all. No. But this policy was forged at the fireside by the supreme commando. The Mammy. And the Mammy says' mind him and he'll leave you the place.' In other words, 'tiochfaidh ar la.' And so, at seventy years of age, Robert Callaghan makes his debut as an air traveller and keen supporter of the sub in the number sixteen jersey. Hah?

LYONS   I wouldn't be bothered arguing with you. You know Robert Callaghan as well as I do, maybe better. He'll do what he wants. And no more than you, Jackie, I know I'll be jibed. I know it'll be said that I'm only looking after him so as I'll get the place. But let it be said. That's not going to stop me looking after a neighbour. Because that's what I should be doing.

PEADAR   Oh, begod, you should. Because you're running out of them fast. You're buying them out. Picking them off, one by one. Like a sniper.

LYONS   Who did I ever buy out?

PEADAR   Who bought our place? My place?

LYONS   Your place?

PEADAR   My place. Who bought that?

LYONS   I did. And your father was damned lucky that I did. Because no one else was interested.

PEADAR   Did you ever ask me if I was interested?

LYONS   Ask you? Ask you? What kind of bullshit is that? Why didn't you buy it at the auction? Wasn't it a Public Auction? And I'll tell you something else, Mister. Mister Big Shot. Do you know why it was put up for Public Auction, even though your father knew I was the only one interested? Hah? He wanted to put it up for Public Auction because he was hoping that one of his sons would buy it. Now.

JACKIE   Back to you in the studio.

PEADAR   That's not true.

LYONS   Well, why don't you ask him? Or is your father not talking to you, either?

PEADAR   Either?

LYONS   As well as your wife.

208

PEADAR	If you don't watch yourself, I'll fucking split you.
LYONS	Now, that's spoken like a true son of Eireann.
PEADAR	I'm warning you, sunshine. This is my town. You're playing away from home. And if I hear you saying that again, I'll remove you from the Leitrim panel for a while. You think you have something. Land, Brid, a number sixteen jersey. Well, if you have something, you'd better mind it because I have nothing and the most dangerous man of all is the man with nothing to lose.
LYONS	And if you have nothing to lose, how will you know if you ever win?
JACKIE	One hundred and eighty.
PEADAR	How will I know if I win? That sounds like one of the Master's.
JACKIE	Maith an fear.
PEADAR	Finish it, Jackie.
JACKIE	Finish what?
PEADAR	Maith an fear. If it was you, the Master would say, 'maith an fear, Mac an Cloig,' so what mac is this man? Hah? Whose son is this?
JACKIE	I don't know.
PEADAR	Dermot, have you the Gaelige? What's the Irish for Paraquat?
DERMOT	What?
JACKIE	*(suddenly alarmed)* Peadar, that's enough.
PEADAR	You see, Dermot, our half orphan wasn't always fatherless. He was not the result of an Immaculate Conception. And his love of the land comes from his late Da. This man's Da, Dermot, was a very progressive farmer. Years before his time, he was. This man's father was killing weeds with Paraquat before any of us even heard of the stuff.
JACKIE	Leave it, Peadar, For God's sake, leave it.
LYONS	No. No. Let him go on. I want to hear this.
PEADAR	And do you see, Dermot, this man's father was also a good neighbour. Like his son is now. Always anxious

to help. And the young widow Flanagan, at the bottom of our mountain, could never have managed without the help that this man's Da gave her. Indeed, Dermot, 'twas said that he was so anxious to help that young widow that he sometimes neglected his own place and this man's Mammy used to be annoyed with him, so she used. But that's neither here nor there. Going back to the weed killer. What no one knew at that time was that that auld paraquat is fierce dangerous stuff, so it is. Deadly. And didn't this man's father swallow a cup of it. By accident. By mistake. Must have thought it was a cup of water. And wasn't Young Lyons here left an orphan. Or a half orphan. And the poor widow Flanagan couldn't get as good a neighbour again and had to sell and move to Sligo. And Dermot, when she sold, do you know who bought?

DERMOT   Him?

PEADAR   Arrah, not at all, Dermot. Sure he was only a cub at the time. No, Dermot, the Mammy bought and thus commenced the putting together of the ranch which this young man commands when he's not stealing women, freeing Ireland or getting piles sitting on the subs bench for Leitrim.
          Lyons rises to go.
          Where are you going?

LYONS   You liar. You fuckin' liar. If you have to stoop that low, then I don't have to go down with you. Not even Clocker...

JACKIE   Whoa. Leave us out of it.

LYONS   Not even Clocker would say a thing like that. Even in fun.

JACKIE   Arrah, Peadar didn't mean anything. Can't you see he's pissed?

PEADAR   Who's pissed?

LYONS   He's pissed? He's pissed? And so he's entitled to the Paddy's pardon, is he? And can that bastard pluck any hen he likes when he's pissed. Plucking hens is great sport, isn't it? But you have to be careful you don't

210

	pluck the wrong hen. Because, Gallagher, did you ever try to put the feathers back on a hen? No? Not easy.
JACKIE	Sure he'll have forgotten he even said it in the morning.
LYONS	But I won't, will I? When will I have forgotten what he said?
	(to Peadar)
	I'll get my bags from your house and I'll stay in the hotel with the team.
PEADAR	There's no need for that.
LYONS	I'd be obliged if you'd leave Robert in tomorrow morning for the coach.
PEADAR	Arrah, Jaysus, man, it was only a bit of craic.
LYONS	*(at door)*
	Is that what it was? Thanks for telling me. I'd never have recognised it.
	He exits.
	Pause
DERMOT	By Jesus, Peadar, you're some outfit.
PEADAR	What?
DERMOT	Arrah, nothing.
PEADAR	Put them up again.
DERMOT	No more brandy for you, Mister. You can have a beer. Jackie?
JACKIE	Lager for me, Dermot.
	Pause
PEADAR	Well, there goes the true Leitrim man. On the run. From the truth. No wonder he's left on the bench.
JACKIE	Ah, shut the fuck up you, will you?
PEADAR	What?
JACKIE	What's wrong with you? What's eating you? Why do you have to bring down everything you come in contact with?
PEADAR	What are you talking about?
JACKIE	Jesus, as long as I've known you. Always needing to be top dog. The King Paddy. Always having to be better than the rest. Even when you met Francine. Lucky bastard. She'd take the eyes out of your head. All the lads drooling over her. But you had to ruin that, too.

	When you got afraid that she might be thought more of than you, you had to humiliate her. Leave her miserable and ashamed in a strange country.
PEADAR	What are you talking about?
JACKIE	The way you treated her when she was expecting the child?
PEADAR	What child?
JACKIE	The child that married ye. Blowing in front of everyone that you were making an honest woman of her. That she'd be. fucked if you didn't marry her because she couldn't go home and she'd be all alone in London. More of the Gallagher craic of having favours owed to you. The poor woman, having to put up with that.
PEADAR	Hi, boy, hold it.
JACKIE	No, I won't hold it. Anytime I ever meet you, you spend your time bawling about how you want to be in Leitrim. And still, you never went home unless you had to. To pay for the conacre. Make sure everyone knew your father couldn't do it on his own.
PEADAR	Jackie, it's not like that. It was never like that.
JACKIE	No? then why did you never go home, say, at Christmas? Why did you never go home when you weren't expected? Hah?
PEADAR	Lynch, you're getting out of your depth here. Remember...
JACKIE	Remember who I am, is it? Remember I'm only one of Clocker's, is it?
PEADAR	No, remember who set you up here. Who gave you the start? How many fuckers in this town did I set on the road? Hah?
JACKIE	Did you not get paid for it? Did we not do any work you gave us?
PEADAR	Ye did.
JACKIE	Well, then we won't be under any compliment to you so. By God, Seamie was right.
PEADAR	Seamie was right about what?
JACKIE	Seamie said when we got the start here, that if we didn't make our own way, you'd begin thinking you

owned us. So we started looking for work off the English. And they laughed at us. And the Paddies laughed at us for letting the English laugh at us. But we stuck at it. And after a while they began to give us work. I don't know why. Maybe it was easier to give it to us than to listen to us looking for it. But we escaped from Gallagher and we owe you nothing now. And that gives you a problem, sunshine. Because you can't go back now and tell Clocker that you're feeding his lads in London. And you'll never be able to say that again.

PEADAR   Jackie, you don't realise. You don't know what it's like for me.

JACKIE   What it's like for you doesn't entitle you to fuck up everyone else. You let your father sell up and come over here and you did nothing since except make him feel guilty for selling the place.

PEADAR   He had to sell the place.

JACKIE   He had not.

PEADAR   He had. You know well it was my mother's dying wish.

JACKIE   For the love of God, Peadar, what woman would want to inflict that on her husband? What wrong was she trying to avenge?

PEADAR   She was doing what she thought was best.

JACKIE   Well, you shouldn't have let it be done. Work with the living, Peadar. Forget the dead. You should never have let Lyons buy that place.

PEADAR   I know that. Jesus. Above all men. That shite.

JACKIE   Wrong, Peadar, wrong. You're wronging Young Lyons the same way you wronged everyone else.

PEADAR   How?

JACKIE   Lyons never wanted to buy your place. He didn't need it. Couldn't afford it. But there was no one else. If he didn't buy it, the forestry was in and that was another twenty acres gone for good. He begged your father not to sell it. He said he's take it on conacre and your father could come over to you and he'd mind it and that maybe yourself or Eamonn would want it later. But no, your father had promised your mother. But he put it up

213

	for Public Auction, hoping you'd buy it. But you were too busy feeling sorry for yourself and fuckin' Young Lyons out of it to read the signs or to talk to anyone about it.
PEADAR	Jackie, is this true?
JACKIE	And now, you shite, you little prick, look what you did to that lad. With your story. Your rumours about his father. Because that's all they are, fuckin' rumours. The only man keeping a bit of light on the side of that mountain and you leave him to go home to face his mother with his heart broken by your stones. His own neighbour.
PEADAR	I said, is it true?
JACKIE	Yes.
PEADAR	How do you know?
JACKIE	How does Mac an Cloig know anything, only from Clocker. What The Master calls the font of all knowledge.
PEADAR	Jesus.
	Pause
DERMOT	Can ye leave it at that, lads?
JACKIE	There'll be no more, Dermot. 'Tis all said now.
DERMOT	Good.
JACKIE	*(brightly)*
	Well, auld stock, what about this place in Kilkenny.
DERMOT	Laugh away, Jackie, but I'll buy it yet.
JACKIE	Believe me, Dermot, I ain't laughing. We have to have a dream. A vision. 'We are such things as dreams are made on.'
DERMOT	Let me guess. Shakespeare?
JACKIE	Aye.
PEADAR	*(softly)*
	The Tempest.
JACKIE	Maith an Fear.
	Pause
PEADAR	What have I done, Jackie? What have I done?
JACKIE	No more nor no less than you've ever done.
PEADAR	I have to fix it. I have to fix it.

JACKIE	How?
PEADAR	I don't know. I don't fuckin' know. But I can't leave it like that.
JACKIE	Maybe you'd be as well to.
PEADAR	No. No. I have to. It has to be stopped.
JACKIE	'Tis easy said. But a lie would have a day's work done while the truth would be having it's breakfast.
PEADAR	All my life, I've done to suit others. I came here for Eamonn. I married for Francine. Stayed here for the kids. And never once, in all that time, did anyone ever ask me what I wanted,
JACKIE	And what did you want, Peadar? Or have you any idea what you want?
PEADAR	I know more about what I don't want because I have more of that. All I know, Jackie, is that this day, I'd swap everything, the business, the house, Francine, the kids, the golf club. I'd swap the whole fuckin' lot for that number sixteen jersey that Young Lyons had on him today. Isn't that daft, Jackie? Hah?
JACKIE	No. Peadar, it's not daft. It's the way you are. Your problem is that you never left Leitrim. You're twenty years in London and you never emigrated. You never gave yourself a chance. You're living in Limbo. Peadar, make your mind up. If you're going to be here, be here. Settle for that.
PEADAR	Oh, God.
JACKIE	Ah, Peadar, you're too hard on yourself, betimes. It'll be alright. It'll be alright.
	Pause
DERMOT	Is he a big farmer?
JACKIE	Who?
DERMOT	Young Lyons.
JACKIE	In Leitrim, Dermot, there are no big farmers. Only small farmers that think they're big farmers. Respectable men, though. Men that would get out of a bath to have a piss. But they're no better nor no worse than any of us. No more than myself or Gallagher there, we all had to be lassoed when we were fourteen

	to put a pair of shoes on us.
	Jackie and Dermot laugh.
	Alright, Peadar?
PEADAR	I was dealt a bad hand.
JACKIE	You were dealt a middling hand. You played it bad.
PEADAR	Did I? Well, look at me now. My wife doesn't speak to me. My father ignores me. My children avoid me. And now Jackie Lynch tells me I destroy everything I touch.
JACKIE	Well, would you like to try playing the hand you're after dealing Young Lyons?
	Pause
	Peadar rises.
PEADAR	I'll see you.
JACKIE	Where are you going?
PEADAR	I'd better start gathering feathers.
JACKIE	Catch your hen first. Go and talk to Young Lyons.
PEADAR	Do you reckon?
JACKIE	You know yourself. Always do the hard part of the job first.
PEADAR	Jesus, Jackie, what'll I say to him?
JACKIE	Tell him you're sorry.
PEADAR	Hah?
JACKIE	You'll catch him off guard if you do. He won't be expecting it.
PEADAR	Do you think?
JACKIE	Peadar, you never had to ask a man for the start in your life. Had you?
PEADAR	No.
JACKIE	Ask him for the start, Peadar. To begin from scratch.
	Pause
PEADAR	I'll leave the car, Dermot. Here's the keys.
	He goes to exit.
JACKIE	Peadar.
PEADAR	What?
JACKIE	*(softly)* Up Leitrim.
PEADAR	*(softly)* Up Leitrim.

Peadar exits.

Pause

DERMOT   Sometimes, Lynch, I think there's more to you than meets the eye.

JACKIE   Oh?

DERMOT   For a fella that says he learned the first line of two hundred poems, you know the middle lines of a good few, too.

JACKIE   Ah, but that's the secret, Dermot.

DERMOT   Secret?

JACKIE   Never let the other fella know what you know. Knowledge is power, Dermot. Now, poor Peadar is after giving away the last bit of knowledge he had to Young Lyons and now he has no more power. He's empty.

DERMOT   One for the road, Jackie?

JACKIE   No, thanks, Derm. I have the gluaistean.

DERMOT   A strange kind of evening.

JACKIE   Aye, strange.

Pause

Strange. But still...

(brightly)

It's not every day that Leitrim beats London. Hah?

He exits, laughing, as lights fade to black.

END

217